CARTOGRAFÍA EVEREST

D1519147

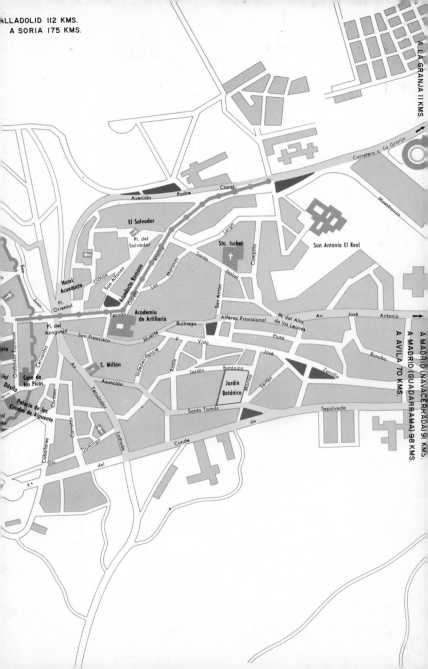

A VALLADOLID 112 KMS.
A SORIA 175 KMS.

A LA GRANJA 11 KMS.

Carretera a La Granja

Maestranza

Avenida   Padre   Claret

El Salvador

Pl. del
Salvador

Sta. Isabel

San Antonio El Real

Larga

Santa

Campillo

Isabel

Hotel
Acueducto

Ochoa

San Alfonso

Acueducto Romano

García

Almira

Los   Morenos

San

Pl.
Oriental

Juan

Fernán

Academia
de Artillería

San Antón

Pl. del
Azoguejo

San Francisco

Muerte

Buitrago

Alférez Provisional

Pl. del Alto
de los Leones

Av.   José   Antonio

A MADRID (NAVACERRADA) 91 KMS.

Cervantes

y

Vida

José

Plata

A MADRID (GUADARRAMA) 98 KMS.

Grabador Espinosa

Caso de
los Picos

S. Millán

Independencia

Roble

Jardín

Rancho

Zorrilla

A AVILA 70 KMS.

Palacio de los
Condes de Alpuente

Carmen

Asunción

Fernández

Jardín
Botánico

Botánico

Morilla

Sortán

Carrera

Domingo

Isadela

Santo Tomás

de

Sepúlveda

Caballares

Costa

del

Conde

P.º

Litografía EVEREST - Avda. San Juan de Sahagún, 5 - LEON

SEGOVIA

TERCERA EDICION

Author: MARIANO GRAU SANZ
Photographs: José M.ª Heredero
Archivo Mas
Oronoz
Official Photograph Service
Paisajes Españoles
Marqués de Sta. M.ª del Villar.

EDITORIAL **EVEREST**

Apartado 339 - LEÓN (España)

Printed in Spain - H. FOURNIER, S.A. - H. Fournier, 19 - Vitoria-1972

A PANORAMIC VIEW OF SEGOVIA

The errosion work done by two currents of water over many thousands of years isolated a large limestone rock, approximately 2,500 meters in perimeter, which as time went on was to become the seat of the city of Segovia. Modern investigations show that the city was most probably founded in 700 BC by the Celts. The great rock is 1,005 meters above sea level in the middle and it is seven kilometers, in a straight line, from the Guadarrama range of mountains.

Even a long time back this crowning city was unable to house its inhabitants, thus giving rise to the external districts, ancient suburbs, mostly to the south of Segovia towards the mountains, although there are also two others to the north and west of the city. It can be assured that the foundation of these suburbs is contemporary in many aspects with the high city, as can be proved by traces of past ages preserved in these districts, and which are contemporary with the ones to be found inside the rocky city of Segovia.

At the foot of the city, towards the south, we find the pure style of the precinct known as Azoguejo, a name perpetuating a remote form of small market. This precinct was famous in the past as a university for the picaresque and is now a point of union between the high Segovia and its external districts, an essential knot of roads and streets bringing all the city communications together. The Aqueduct stretches over this famous site, with the magnificent theory of its unequalled arches, an impressive link between the distant past and the reality of the present, gregarian and multiform.

Segovia is then a high acropolis, of medieval design, with streets, squares and monuments of a secular type, where history and legend are to be found at every corner; but this is also true of the districts outside the walls, which are more populous than the city itself, where the vestiges of remote times are to be found side by side with variegated constructions corresponding to the growing rythm of the increase in population and the upward trend of the industrial life in search of new outlets.

Artistically and archeologically Segovia is a Museum housing treasures of all periods and styles, as a consequence of a full history of important events.

Partial view of Segovia from the Veracruz. ⟶

THE THOUSAND YEAR OLD AQUEDUCT

This famous monument, an example without equivalent on earth, is like an old craftsman who still continues to carry out the profession for which he was meant after all these centuries: it was built for the purpose of bringing water to the city on its thousand year old back. It is 728 meters long and its maximum height over Azoguejo is 29 meters. It consists of a first section of simple arches which begins close to the San Ildefonso road and finishes in the Plaza de Diaz Sanz; there are 75 arches in this section, gradually growing in size. This stretch is followed by a section of double arches to counteract a more pronounced slope, consisting of 88 arches; 4 more simple arches inside the walls should be added to the latter. The total number of arches in the Roman Aqueduct is 167. Its great granite rocks are naturally placed, without any type of mortar whatsoever.

The first section of simple arches contains 36 of these arches which offer a certain novelty with regard to the reamining ones; the pointed curve. These arches were redone in the 15th century by Fr. Juan de Escobedo, a Jerome monk from El Parral, in order to restore the section of the Aqueduct destroyed by al-Mamum, the Moorish king of Toledo, in 1072. Some other arches in the same sector were also restored later, but the rest are all the original ones.

The exact period when this famous monument was built is unknown although modern investigations situate its construction in the second half of the 1st century and beginning of the 2nd century, corresponding to the reigns of the emperors Vespasianus and Trajan. The modillion to be found over the Azoguejo, under the niches, once held the bronze letters, which referred to the Aqueduct's foundation. and which Juan de Valdés in his work «Diálogo de la Lengua» (Dialogue on the language) says that some still existed at the time of the publication of the book in 1527.

Until 1884 the water passed through a canal carved out on the top part of the aqueduct and in that year it stopped fulfilling the mission it had carried out for so many centuries. However, in 1928 it once more took up its secular mission, although the water runs through a wide pipe, installed in the afore-mentioned canal, supplying the higher part of the city.

The Aqueduct, the heraldic shield of Segovia, is one of the monuments of the best artistic and archeological category to be found today in the world.

Aerial view of Segovia.

Detail of the Postigo arches with a glimpse of San Justo in the background.

← The smooth angular harmony of the thousand year old Aqueduct.

Two views of the Aqueduct over the Azoguejo square

THE CASTLE

To the west of the city, the regal castle stands out on the sharp ridge where the rock supporting the higher part of Segovia ends, on the beds of river Eresma and the stream Clamores, which join further down. This is perhaps the most finished of all Spanish castles, forming a perspective of magnificent quality, and has been considered as one of the famous landscapes of the world.

On this ridge of rock, dominating the entrances into the valley, there must have been another lookout or fort for watching and defending, which existed from very remote times. It is no longer doubted today that the Romans had one and it is also not unreasonable to state that the Arabs also had a similar type of stronghold, as the Castle is already mentioned in 12th century manuscripts, after the conquest of the city by Alfonso VI.

The monarchs of Castile lived there frequently, extending and enriching the rooms, in accordance with the needs of the times. They were Alfonso VIII, Alfonso X, Juan II, Enrique IV and the Catholic Kings. Philip II substituted in the second half of the 16th century the old arms courtyard for the renaissance one, which can be seen today and changed the old tiled roofs for the present slate ones.

It is natural that this magnificent castle should be the scene of many important events over the centuries: Parliament was held here in 1256, 1342, 1343, 1389 and 1532; Isabel the Catholic Queen went out from here on 13th December 1474 to be crowned Queen of Castile, on the decision of the Council of Segovia, in the porch of the church of St. Michael; Philip II was married to Ana of Austria on 12th November 1570 in the Kings' Hall in the castle. It was a state prison in the 16th, 17th and 18th centuries, and famous personages, such as the Duke of Medinaceli, the Marquis of Ayamonte, the Baron of Riperda, the Duke of Guisa, the adventurer Lupati, etc., passed through its rooms as prisoners.

In 1764, Charles III established the Royal Artillery College in the Castle and in March 1862 a fire destroyed a great part of this magnificent fortress and palace of the Kings of Castile, wiping out the great wealth of art which had been accumulated inside the walls. Twenty years later the Castle was restored for the purpose of installing the General Military Archives in its rooms.

The Alcazar. ⟶

The Alcazar from the entrance gardens.

The characteristic Clock courtyard.

The main courtyard in the Alcazar.

Galley chamber.

Throne room.

Alcazar. Homage tower. ⟶

THE ROYAL ROOMS

In 1940 a project was undertaken for restoring the rooms in the Alcazar to their natural state, bringing out the elements covered up during the restoration after the fire or substituting them for more appropriate ones in the case of a total loss. The restoration began with the Throne Room, built in 1456 by Henry IV, by completing the beautiful Moorish frieze and installing a 15th century caissoned ceiling, which came from Urones de Castroponce in the province of Valladolid.

Then the «Galley Chamber» was restored. It was given this name on account of the old caissoned ceiling which imitated the hull of a galley destroyed by fire in 1862. In this room, built by catherine of Lancaster in 1412, gour small windows of the XIV century were left in view that mark what was the limit of the Alcazar in that area. They also discovered and restored the frieze that surrounds the room.

The Pine-cone Room, the work of Henry IV done in 1452, given this name on account of the pinecones used in the decoration of the caissoned ceiling, was restored later, using the same principals as on previous occasions. The frieze here was also discovered and restored and the ceiling was redone in accordance with the name given to the room. Then the «King's Bedroom» was restored, installing two Moorish doors, donated by the Count of Almodovar, a copy of the ones in what was Henry IV's palace.

Finally, restoration work was carried out on the staircase and rooms in King John II's turret, as well as in the Chapel. The Chapel has also been given a magnificent altarpiece of the time of the Catholic Kings, expertly restored by the city's artist, Garcia Ayuso; a very characteristic caissoned ceiling, from Cedillo de la Torre in the province of Segovia, has also been installed in the Chapel and its walls have been covered with valuable damask decorated with Jacobean motifs.

It is very interesting to note that the Throne Room, the Galley Chamber and the Pine-cone Room, as well as the Chapel, have all been provided with beautiful glass cases, projected over vignettes of the «Palace Code» by the great Segovian glassblower Carlos Muñoz de Pablos, who also painted a mural of large proportions in the Galley Chamber, representing the Coronation of Isabel the Catholic Queen. The Castle Patronage has enhanced the rooms with furniture and effects of an authenticera, and has also installed an artillery museum.

King's bedroom. →

Armoury room.

The Cathedral from the Pinarillo.

THE QUEEN OF THE CATHEDRALS

The former cathedral of St. Mary's, a 12th century construction was situated in what are now the Castle gardens and was partly destroyed during the Peoples' War in 1521; four years later the construction of the present Cathedral was begun, the last of the Gothic style in Spain. One hundred houses and an old convent of Clarissa Nuns had to be destroyed for the cathedral's construction. The work was done in accordance with the plans drawn up by Juan Gil de Hontañón, the architect of the new cathedral in Salamanca.

The inauguration took place on 15th August 1558, thirty three years after the work began, when the cathedral was built as far as the transept, with great ceremonies, rejoicings and illuminations. The high tower —twelve metres higher than it is today— stood out against the sky with its great Gothic needle, made of mahogany from America, and heat guilded lead. Whilst the Cathedral was being built, the 15th century Gothic cloister of the former cathedral was transferred to the new site, together with the choirstalls, of the same period, which were saved from destruction.

In 1563 aproject was undertaken to build the High Chapel, basilica and apse, under the direction of Rodrigo Gil de Hontañón, the original architect's son, who had already died. The former skilfully and intelligently carried out the work and the building was completed bit by bit later.

In 1614 lightning destroyed the great needle of the tower, also setting light to the Cathedral roofs, as splinters of burning wood from the tower were scattered by a violent hurrican, thus placing the new building in great danger. Five years later, Juan de Mugaguren restored the tower, giving it its present structure and cutting 12 meters off its former height. About this time, Pedro de Brizuela carved the San Frutos door and some years later the so called «Sagrario Chapel» was added to the church. The Cathedral was consecrated in 1768 and its dimensions are: 105 meters long, 50 wide and 33 high in the central nave; the tower is 88 meters high. It has been named «The Queen of the Cathedrals» on account of its slim, graceful and luminous outlines.

Right from the start of the work up to the inauguration of the Cathedral, the people of Segovia took part in the construction, either by working or by contributing economically, in an enthusiastic and active manner.

Cathedral. View of the apse and the transept.

← The Cathedral and the old Jewish quarter.

IN AND ABOUT THE NAVES

We shall very briefly, as the subject is a lengthy one, refer to various works of art, of exceptional quality, housed in the Cathedral. We shall begin with the first chapel, on the right, beyond the San Frutos door. It is called «Piedad» and contains an impressive altarpiece carved in 1571 by Juan de Juni. In front of the latter there is a Flemish tryptych of large proportions, painted by Ambrosius Benson at the beginning of the 16th century. It is one of the artist's main works.

The third chapel in this section, St. Cosme and St. Damian, contains a statue of the Virgin by Gregorio Fernandez, of exceptional value. The last chapel, La Concepcion, houses a good collection of pictures of undoubtable merit, some being by Ries. It also has a splendid carved mahogany grille. On the other side, in front of these chapels, in the second one, there is a reclining Christ by Gregorio Fernandez, which is classified as one of his best works and is taken out in the procession on Good Friday night; and in the next door chapel, St. Barbara, there is baptismal font donated to the old Cathedral by Enrique IV. In the following chapel, Santiago, there is a good picture by Alonso de Herrera, a Segovian painter of the 17th century, which had been attributed for a long time to Pantoja de la Cruz.

The Sagrario Chapel exhibits a Crucifix by Pereira, beautifully executed and framed in an artistic ceramic altar by Daniel Zuloaga. In the High Chapel there is a neo-classical altarpiece in marble and bronze, by Sabatini, and a statue of the Virgin of Peace, donated to the old Cathedral by Enrique IV. The latter is a 13th century carving, covered in silver, which belonged to Fernando III. On the arm of the transept, which is closed off by the St. Jeroteo door, there is a Crucifixion, also of the 13th century, which belonged to the old Cathedral.

As we have already said, the choirstalls, carved during the second half of the 15th century, were transferred to the present Cathedral, when it was being built. They were donated by Bishop Juan de Arias Davila.

The «Piedad» and «Cristo del Consuelo» chapels are closed off by two Plateresque grilles by Francisco de Salamanca, which incorporated the one from the High Chapel in the old Cathedral. Special mention should be made to the Cathedral's artistic stained-glass, some primitive Flemish and others of the 17th century, as well as to the two 18th century organs.

Gosple's nave. —

Christ in Agony, called Lozoya's Christ,

Burial of Christ by Juan de Juni (1571).

Reclining Christ by Gregorio Fernandez.

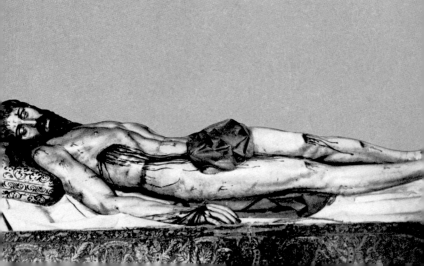

The Annunciation on the back of the doors of the
A. Benson tryptych.

Tryptych by A. Benson (16th c.).

16th c. tryptych in the Cathedral Museum.

View of the cloister, which also belonged to the old Cathedral.

Gothic baptismal font, Virgin of Peace (13th c.), view of the choir and cloister door originally from the old Cathedral.

MUSEUM AND CAPITULAR CHAMBER

In the «Cristo del Consuelo» Chapel, in which we find the tombs of the bishops Don Raimundo de Losana and Don Diego de Covarrubias, there is a Gothic 15th century door, which opens on to the Cloister. The latter was built at the same time by Juan Guas and donated to the old Cathedral by Enrique IV. It was then transferred and erected on its present site by Juan Campero. The cloister is in the Gothic style of the end of the 15th century, perhaps a little too ornate, but suggestive and evocative.

Part of the Cathedral Museum is housed in the chapel to be found in the base of the tower. There are some paintings attributed to Morales, Berruguete, Van Eyck, etc.; several interesting reliquaries, especially one by Benvenuto Cellini; a 13th century statue of the Virgin and Child in her lap and valuable 16th and 17th century church vestments. The cart used in the Corpus Christi procession, the top part of which is carved in silver by Ramon Gonzalez, is also on view. In the centre of the chapel, there is the tomb of the infante Don Pedro, son of Enrique II, who fell from the arms of his nurse over the castle walls. He was buried before in the old Cathedral.

The rest of the Museum is housed in another room on top of the Capitular Chamber. It contains an extraordinary collection of incunabulae of the second half of the 15th century, some of the best in Spain; splendid church robes; valuable reliquaries; good paintings, statues and other works of art are also to be found here along with round robbins, ancient royal deeds and a collection of coins. The Cathedral archives, which are of great documental importance, are also housed here.

The Capitular Chamber is a beautiful, nobly proportioned room, exhibiting a magnificent collection of Gobelin tapestries, which represent scenes from the life of Queen Zenobia. Special mention should be made to the caissoned ceiling in this room, exquisitely carved and gilded, which enhances the tapestries. A 16th century Christ Crucified holds out its pain stricken arms on the back walls.

As we come out of the Capitular Chamber we come face to face with a frightening picture by Valdes Leal and opposite there is a large canvas by Esquivel. There are some good tapestries of undoubtable merit hanging on the staircase leading to the Museum. Outside, ont the Cloister walls, we find the tomb of Marial del Salto, the Jewess who was flung over the cliff, which is seeped in legend.

Cathedral Museum. Monastrance float used at Corpus (17th c.).

San Andres gateway in the wall.

Cathedral. View of the apse. ⟶

THE WALL AND ITS GATES

The wall, with its warlike semblance, follows the contours of the rock on which the city is founded and a stretch of some 2,500 meters long hems in the high part of the city. This wall dates back to the time of the conquest of Segovia —at the end of the 11th century— and to the following century, although it was both restored and added to at later dates. At various points in the embattled wall, there are Roman stelas and stones with such names as Sextus Severus and Publius Juvenal Juvenalis.

Seven gates and seven wicket gates or posterns opened up in the wall. Of the former, four were demolished in the last century and of the latter, there are two which have been bricked in and one still open, restored in 1947. The gates which were demolished were known as «Sol», «La Luna», «San Martin» and «San Juan», the ones still in existence being «San Cebrian», «Santiago» and «San Andres». The first of the latter, perhaps the simplest and most suggestive, opens out on to the Eresma valley and is in the oldest sector of the wall, still imposing its warlike nature on the way up to the city. A stone cross stands out, built on an outcrop of rocks towards the end of the 16th century, on the otherside of the San Cebrian gateway.

The Santiago gate, also opening out onto the Eresma valley, is a Mudejar type structure, with horseshoe arches and strong and arrogant in aspect. To the west the wall continues for quite a way up to the castle. However, in the opposite direction, the wall has fallen down on account of a landslide which occurred several years ago.

The San Andres gate, which gives access to the old Jewish quarter, looks out on to the Clamores stream and was restored at the time of Charles I. The wall then continues in a well preserved stretch, restored in the Mudejar style. Inside the San Andres gateway, there is a plaque recording that the cheat Pablos passed through this territory and above there is a niche dedicated to the Virgin.

Both the San Andres gate and the immediate wall have been recently restored by the Fine Arts Board.

San Cebrian gateway, from inside the wall. ⟶

Santiago gate, in the Eresma valley.

THE ROMANIC CHURCHES (I)

Segovia contained at one time thirty 11th, 12th and 13th century romanic churches, which goes to show the city's importance during the early Middle Ages. At present twelve of these Romanic churches are open for worship and four others house various cultural and artistic services. Two others, El Salvador and Santa Eulalia, were reformed in the 16th and 17th centuries on the primitive Romanic foundations and still preserve some of the old elements.

In this Romanic set up which is so characteristic of Segovia, there are various first category churches which are eloquent artistic and historical reminders of events seeped in significance for the city and its well-fare over the times. The first of these churches is San Millan, which presides over the district of the same name, a former Moorish Quarter. It was built in the 12th century over what would appear to be another church, to which the present tower belonged. The church has three naves, with four apses and two splendid porches and the two magnificent main and south doors. The interior of the apse of the central nave has beautiful arches, which until recently were hidden behind a large altarpiece, when some noteworthy paintings were discovered on the entrance arch to the high chapel. On account of the church's structure and disposition it has been compared with the Jaca cathedral. The tower was recently restored by the Fine Arts Board. Two carvings by the Segovian sculpture, Aniceto Marinas who lived in the district, are kept in the church, which also has some fine stained glass by the artist Muñoz de Pablos.

«La Trinidad», situated in the little square of the same name, is another of the important Romanic churches, built in the 12th century on the remains of another undoubtedly Mozarab church. As in the case of San Millan, the apse in the nave is composed of beautiful arches inside which were discovered twenty years ago. There is a Gothic chapel attached of the Campo and Trinidad class, with the characteristic access arch and the exceptional altarpiece of a good old design on one side. The wonderful picture by Ambrosious Benson of the Holy Face is also on view. This beautiful church of the Trinity, with its slim porch and impressive doors, is in a corner full of the past, close to the Dominican convent.

San Millan church (12th c.).

Church of La Trinidad. Holy Face by A. Benson.

THE ROMANIC CHURCHES (II)

The church of San Martin presides over one of the most interesting spots in Segovia — the graded perspective of the squares of San Martin and Medina del Campo. This 12th century Romanic church has two superb porches and magnificent doors, the exterior one being a most interesting example with sculptures serving as columns. The church also has two apses, one of them only just recently discovered, as the central one had disappeared during one of the extensions to the church. Inside there are several interesting chapels with tombs, especially the Herrera family chapel which has a lovely altarpiece. Among the valuable statues kept in this church, the following are of exceptional quality: St. Francis of Assisi by Pedro de Mena; a reclining Christ by Gregorio Fernandez, a deeply moving work; a Flemish tryptych, etc.

The church of «La Veracruz» or «Los Templarios» is situated close to the St. Marcos district, on the edge of the Zamarramala road. It was built by the Templerian Knights at the beginning of the 13th century and when the order was dissolved, it went into the hands of the Maltese Order, who owned it until the end of the 17th century. It was then abandoned only surviving by a real miracle until 1845 when it was saved under the first project undertaken by the Provincial Commission for Monuments. It only has one nave which revolvers round a central temple, in which the stone table used by the knights for their arms is kept. The church is in the shape of a twelve sided polygon, although the tower is later. In 1951 it was returned to the Maltese Order, who restored it, discovering very interesting old paintings in the walls. It has been a National Monument since 1919.

San Lorenzo is another Romanic church of undoubtable importance. It presides over the district of the same name, in the river Eresma valley, and is surrounded by ancient characteristic buildings, giving the square a vigorous Castilian savour. Three magnificent apses, with the undeniable quality of 12th century Romanic art, and a superb porch, put the church in a very high category, even more accentuated by the tower, which is the city's only example of bricks used in the Romanic style. We should mention here a tryptych which is on view in the apse chapel on the same side as the Epistle chapel and is the work of the carver, Benito Giralte and the painter Rodrigo de Segovia.

The great Dominican theologian Domingo Soto was born in this quarter of San Lorenzo, a district of secular gardens.

Church of La Trinidad (12th c.).

Capitals from the San Martin porch.

San Martin porch.

San Martin. St. Francis carved by Pedro de Mena, sculptures on
the doorway and Reclining Christ by Gregorio Fernandez.

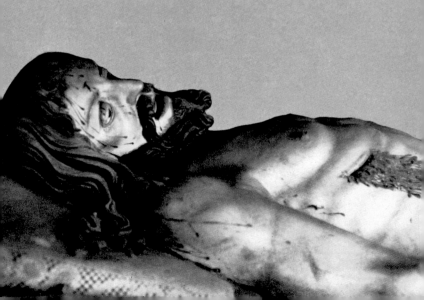

Church of the Templarios or Veracruz. Exterior and
interior views (1208).

THE ROMANIC CHURCHES (III)

On the northern slopes of the town, a Romanic tower of superb design towers gracefully above the conglomeration of the city's rooftops: it is the tower of the church of San Esteban and is known as «the Queen of the Bizantine towers». Only the tower and porch remain of the primitive construction of the church, which is situated in the square of the same name. But these two elements, on their own, are examples of the highest quality. The tower consists of four sections, which are built on to a base of the same height as the church nave and is topped by a slate spire and measures a total of 53 meters. On account of a fire in the old spire in 1896, the tower was dismantled as far as the beginning of the perforated windows and the project for rebuilding it was finally completed in 1928. The porch was also restored after it was damaged when the scaffolding collapsed. Inside a 13th century crucifix, which is enveloped in the aura of a legend similar to the one attached to the «Cristo de la Vega» in Toledo, is worshipped. The tower of San Esteban church has been a National Monument since 1896.

The Romanic church of San Justo, situated in the district of the same name outside the city walls, has acquired an exceptional artistic importance over the last few years. During the restoration work carried out on the Church by the Caja de Ahorros de Segovia, important discoveries were made, such as an exquisitely worked Romanic lintel; windows and other elements which had been covered up. However, what really makes this church so exceptional today is a collection of 12th century Romanic paintings, covering the interior of the apse and vault. This collection, which had lain forgotten under layer of lime, was discovered during the restoration work. This collection is a valuable example of Romanic pictoric art similar to the ones in Berlanga de Duero, Leon and Madderuelo and has been faithfully restored by the Gudiol brothers. The paintings represent Christ encircled by a halo and the old men of the Apocalypse in the sky. On both sides of the figure of Christ, there are scenes from the Passion and His Death, together with other pictoric themes, which are unusual in this type of Romanic painting.

San Justo has a lovely tower, the final section of which is disfigured; it also has a characteristic apse and a Romanic door. Inside, there is a 13th century reclining Christ, known as «Christ of the Gascones» and also the origin of a moving legend. St. Alfonso Rodriguez was baptized here.

Church of San Lorenzo. Top end and tower.

Tower and top end of church of San Justo.

Cross in the church of San Esteban (13th c.).⟶

OTHER VESTIGES OF ROMANIC ART

On account of the whimsical planning of the Segovian streets, both inside the walls and in the external districts, there are still other Romanic churches, which although they may not come up to the standard of the ones already described, offer points of interest. In the top part of the city, there is the church of San Andres, in the Plaza de la Merced, with a magnificent apse and an interesting tower; inside there is a good altarpiece by Mateo Inverto with excellent paintings by Alonso de Herrera and a Virgin of exceptional value. The church of San Sebastian, in the square of the same name, has a very good apse, a characteristic doorway and a reformed tower. It was once the coiners' parish church.

The church of San Clemente is situated outside the city walls and its apse is essentially different to other Romanic apses; it still preserves the old doors and the remains of a porch. The church of St. Thomas also has an old apse and some interesting paintings inside. The church of San Marcos, which is situated in a typical district of the same name, considered as the oldest in Segovia, has a Crucifix of some merit and a St. Jerome which is reminiscent of the hand of Berruguete. As we have already indicated in a previous chapter, there are vestiges of Romanic art in the churches of Santa Eulalia and El Salvador.

But other vestiges of Romanic art can still be seen in and about the city, such as for example the apses of the no longer existing churches of San Blas and San Gil, in the Eresma valley, and another reformed apse in the San Vicente Convent in the San Lorenzo Quarter. In another architectural sphere, it is not unusual to come up against Romanic doorways in various buildings, especially in the San Esteban districts and in the streets forming the area formerly known as «Las Canongias». This famous area, also known as «La Claustra» in the past, was inhabited by all the personnel connected with the old Cathedral. There was once an inner wall with three doors which were closed at curfew, thus isolating this quarter from the rest of the city. This area known as «La Claustra» was granted some important privileges, including the right to give asylum. Of the three aforementioned doors, only one, the «Canongia vieja» still exists in a street now called «calle de Velarde». The other two were demolished in 1570, when Philip II and Ana of Austria were married, to make way for the royal procession.

Tower and apse of the church of San Andres. ──▶

◀── Church of San Esteban.

Santo Tomas. Apse and tower.

Romanic entrance to the Casa de los Linajes.

Romanic entrance to the former Canongias district.

La Claustra gateway.

CHURCHES USED FOR OTHER PURPOSES

We mentioned previously that four of the Romanic churches in Segovia were used for artistic and cultural activities. The most important one is San Juan de los Caballeros, which is the head-quarters of the Zuloaga Museum and School of Ceramics. It is a 12th century construction built on an older one, of which the apse of the central nave was part. It has splendid doors, a porch, three apses and a tower recently restored by the Fine Arts Board. The church was left abandoned in the last century and the great ceramic artist, Daniel Zuloaga, acquired it in 1905 and converted it into his studio and ceramic workshop. The Museum contains some valuable pieces of artistic ceramics and paintings by Daniel and Ignacio Zuloaga. Diego de Colmenares, Segovia's historian, was the church's parish priest in the 17th century and his tomb is in the apse by the lectern.

San Quirce is another of the churches abandoned during the last century and used afterwards for different purposes. In 1927 when it was in a semi-ruined condition, it was acquired by the Universidad Popular Segoviana who restored it making it into a conference hall and a circulating public library'. In 1949, the then governor of the province, Perez Villanueva, donated a large platform, benches and other effects and not very long ago the Caja de Ahorros de Segovia restored the mutilated tower and the main door. It now houses the San Quirce Accademy of History and Art, which is dependent upon the Higher Board of Scientific Investigations. Enrique IV's chronicler, Diego Enriquez del Castillo, was buried in this church.

San Nicolas, situated in the characteristic square of the same name, is also a 12th century Romanic church, with good apses and a tower very much in style. It was restored several years ago and a 14th century tomb, with the mummy of a man and curious paintings on the tomb's roof, was discovered inside one of the apses. The outer porch was added during the time of the said works and now houses a Primary School.

Finally, San Pedro de los Picos, of which only the apse and part of the nave·still stood, has been recently restored by the Conde de Melgar as an artistic studio and exhibition room for the countess's paintings, who is an artist of some note. It is situated close to the inner patrol road, near the Santiago gate, in a very typical setting.

Room in the Zuloaga Museum. ⊢

San Juan de los Caballeros, today the Zuloaga Museum.

San Pedro de los Picos and San Quirce, today the Accademy of History and Art.

CHURCHES OF OTHER PERIODS

The old Romanic church of San Miguel, in the porch of which Isabel the Catholic Queen was crowned queen on 13th December 1474 on the decision of the Council of Segovia, after she had been proclaimed by the same council, was situated in the central part of the Plaza Mayor. The old church collapsed in 1532 and not long after, a project was undertaken for building the present church of San Miguel, moving its situation further south to widen the square. The craftsmen who were then building the Cathedral must have intervened in the construction of this church on account of its characteristics. It has a magnificent Gothic nave and altarpiece at the high altar, which was done in 1672 by Jose de Ferreras inaccordance with plans by Juan de Lobera.

We pick out from the chapels in the church the one named after the governor Diego de Rueda, which has some interesting tombs and the one which houses the tomb of the famous doctor who tended popes and kings, Dr. Andres Laguna, who died in 1560. On the gable-wall in the church façade there are some Romanic figures and carved stones which came from the original San Miguel church.

The Plaza del Seminario is heightened by the majestic granite façade of what was the church of the Jesuit monastery, built in the Escorial style of the 16th century and which today belongs to the Diocesan Seminary. It undoubtedly gives class to the square, with its amply proportioned façade, cushioned ashlars and round stone balls. The church has three naves and its altarpiece is of interest. There is a courtyard worthy of note, the work of Juan de Mugaguren in the 17th century, in the adjoining building which was the Jesuit Monastery and which is now the Diocesan Seminary. The building has recently been subjected to reforms and important extensions. The great Suarez was a teacher here and the exquisite poet Alonso de Ledesma of Segovia was buried in the church.

The Corpus Christi Convent, in the square of the same name, is of special interest on account of its history. In the 13th century it was a Hebrew synagogue, similar to Santa Maria la Blanca in Toledo. It was raised to the ground by fire in 1899. It was later reconstructed on similar lines, although it was impossible to redo many of the details. In 1410 the supernatural event known as «the miracle of the Synagogue» took place here. It was then converted into a Catholic church and is now a convent for Franciscan Clarissa nuns.

Altarpiece in the church of San Miguel. —

Façade of the Diocesan Seminary church,
which was once a Jesuit monastery.

Interior of the Corpus Christi church,
a foremer synagogue.

FAMOUS MONASTERIES (I)

The 15th century, a golden one in many respects for Segovia, left the city with first class religious buildings, almost all of which are still standing today. There are two such constructions in the Eresma valley: El Parral Monastery and Santa Cruz la Real. The former, which was built by Juan Guas during the second half of the 15th century, is in the Gothic style of the end of the 15th century; the plateresque tower, designed by Juan Campero, is 16th century. The altarpiece at the high altar, also a 16th century work, is superb and so are the side tombs, with the kneeling figure of D. Juan Pacheco, the marquis of Villena and Doña Maria Portocarrero, his wife. Close to the sacristy door, which is worthy of note, we find the tomb of Doña Beatriz Pacheco, the countess of Medellin, daughter of the Marquis of Villena. The monastery belonged to the Jerome Order and was abandoned when the Order was disbanded in 1835 and underwent many difficult changes. In 1927 the Order or St. Jerome was once more reborn inside its venerable walls and is now the headquarters of the Order. It has been restored on several occasions, although a great deal still remains to be done in this respect. The following all helped Juan Guas in the building of the monastery: his brother Bonifacio; Salvador de Almonacid, a sculptor; Juan de Ruesgas, carver; Juan Gallego, author of the plans and other artists. The altarpiece is by Juan Rodriguez, Blas Hernandez and Jeronimo Pellicer. El Parral has been a National Monument since 1914.

During the beginning of the 13th century, Santo Domingo de Guzman founded his first Spanish order under the name of Order de Predicadores de Segovia, over the same cave where he had undergone rigurous penitence and which was called Santa Cruz la Real. At the end of the 15th century, the Catholic Kings built the present building, extending and improving the original foundations. It would appear that on account of some of the details the work was done by Juan Guas and his collaboraters. On the exterior cornice of the nave, we find the «Tanto Monta» of the Catholic Kings which is repeated in carved letters. Airy Gothic needles and a beautiful exquisitely carved doorway give this interesting building an artistic silhouette. The cave in which Santo Domingo lived during the 13th century can still be seen in the monastery gardens.

Santa Cruz la Real, close to the Segovia-Zamora road, and not far from the San Lorenzo district, at the foot of the wall, was abandoned during the last century. It was later adjudicated to the Deputation Provincial to be used as a Charity Home

El Parral Monastery. Small cloister. ➞

El Parral. Altarpiece by Juan Rodriguez, Blas Hernandez
and Jeronimo Pellicer (16th c.).

San Justo. Polychromed Romanic tympanum.

General view of the Parral Monastery.

Enrique IV, master of Segovia when he was 14 years old, had built, when he was still a prince, a holiday palace which was full of beautiful Gothic and Moorish details in the district then called «El Campillo», to the south of the city. Many years later, he handed the palace over to the Order of Franciscanos Observantes, who established their monastery in it, under the name of San Antonio el Real; and in 1488 when the monks moved to the monastery of San Francisco —today the Artillery Accademy— it was occupied by the Santa Clara nuns, who still use it.

As it was a closed order, only its very beautiful church was known to the general public. However, the public is now permitted to visit certain parts of the convent at stated times. The various parts on view are a synthesis of the riches contained in the convent. The church has a very simply executed Gothic doorway and there is an impressively beautiful caissoned ceiling, Moorish in design, in the High Chapel vault. There is a Flemish crucifixion scene on the wall by the side of the Epistle, which is made up of several polychromed carved figures. The whole work is astonishing on account of its exceptional qualiti.

Beyond the sacristy, which has a curious caissoned ceiling, we go into the part of the Monastery which is today opened to the public. This consists of the gallery surrounding a cloister and the rooms which open on to same. There is another beautiful caissoned ceiling in the gallery, together with different statues, and paintings of various periods, as well as a whitewashed Gothic doorway. There are three Flemish tryptychs of the Utrech school at different points in the gallery. They are dated in the second half of the 15th century and according to the opinion of Dutch specialists they are unique examples. The central part of these tryptyches is sculptured ·and the side panels are painted, the latter requiring a certain amount of restoration. You may also visit the Refrectory, with an interesting pulpit of the time of Enrique IV; the capitular chamber, with a lovely caissoned ceiling and rich church vestments, and what was the Royal Chamber, the caissoned ceiling of which is exquisitely executed.

Close to San Antonio el Real, we find the Convent of Santa Isabel, in the street of the same name, also 15th century Gothic in style, with an interesting church with good artistic details. It is a closed order convent.

Santa Cruz la Real. Church door, —
of the Juan Guas school (15th c.).

Monastery of San Antonio el Real. Exterior and Mudejar caissoned ceiling in the High Chapel.

San Antonio el Real. Flemish Calvary.

Convent of Santa Isabel. Virgin of the milk (16th c.).

SANTA TERESA DE JESUS AND SAN JUAN DE LA CRUZ

One day in the month of March in 1574, mother Teresa de Jesus, accompanied by Fr. Juan de la Cruz and Fr. Julian de Avila, reached Segovia to carry out what was to be her ninth foundation. On the 19th of the said month, the first mass was said by San Juan de la Cruz in the convent of the Order of the Carmelitas Descalzas, situated in a house which is today no. 1 of the Calle de Daoiz. However this event was forcibly interrupted by the Bishopric. In the following September the convent was transferred to a mansion also in the same street, where it still is today. This move was hotly opposed by the Order of the Mercedarios who lived in the monastery in front and there were some difficulties with the Cathedral Council on a matter of rent, but these were finally smoothed out. The house where the Order was originally founded still preserves the turner's lathe and the caissoned ceiling of what was the chapel. Santa Teresa brought the nuns of the Pastrana convent, which had been closed shortly before, to the convent in Segovia.

Twelve years later, San Juan de la Cruz, with the help of Doña Ana de Peñalosa, completed the founding of the convent for the Carmelitas Descalzas Order at the same place in the Eresma Valley where the Trinitarians of Santa Maria de Rocamador had their convent until a few years before. San Juan de la Cruz remained in Segovia as Prior of the Convent during 1588, 89, 90 and the beginning of 1591. A few months after he left Segovia, San Juan de la Cruz died in Ubeda and two years after his death, his body was transferred to Segovia to be buried in the convent which he himself had founded. The convent still preserves the simple tomb in which his body was laid to rest until he was made a Saint and his body transferred to the high altar. He now lies in a sumptuous tomb, which was made in 1926, in the coffer set on top of the mausoleum, surrounded by statues of the Carmelite saints.

In the convent garden, which is in a spot called «Peñas Grajeras», there is a small chapel called after Santa Teresa, with a cypress tree, now dead, which San Juan de la Cruz planted; farther down there is a bigger chapel over the cave where the Saint used to retire to meditate and which is the monks' cemetery. In the church there is a small museum of Carmelite trophies, such as a picture of Jesus, who, according to tradition, spoke to San Juan de la Cruz, and some manuscripts and relics.

Entrance to the convent founded by Santa Teresa de Jesus. ⟶

Carmelitas Descalzos convent. Panoramic view and tomb
of San Juan de la Cruz.

THE OLD PALACES

If we go up through Segovia via the calle de San Juan, we come to a gardened square flanked by old palaces. The first one, on the left, built on the wall with a fortified tower, has a large granite door with huge keystones and inside there is a splendid courtyard which displays beautiful Moorish style windows with a pillar down the middle. It is a 15th century palace and belonged to the Marques de Moya and is usually called «Casa de Segovia» and also «Casa de las Cadenas»; its strong walls once supported the city wall door, known as San Juan which was demolished in 1886. It once had its own surrounding wall, of which some still stands, and the palace has been recently restored by its owner, the architect Señor Escorial.

In front is the palace belonging to the Marques de Lozoya, and which once belonged to the Caceres family. It has a beautiful 13th century Romanic entrance and beyond the characteristic hall, there is a Gothic courtyard of noble design. This palace, which has extensive gardens on the wall, contains some good works of art and several very sumptuous rooms. In the wall looking on to the Calle de San Juan there is a classic niche which contains a 13th century carved Virgin, which once stood in the demolished gateway.

Close to the Marques de Lozoya's palace we find the palace which belonged to Juan de Contreras in the 15th century and which was inhabited at the end of the last century and beginning of this one by the Conde de Cheste, after whom the square is named. It has a Gothic entrance and some years ago when work was being done on the palace, another door and a beautiful Moorish style window were discovered. It is now a school run by the MM. Concepcionistas Order and the interior has been changed a great deal.

On the other side the square is flanked by the palace which belonged to the Quintanar family, also in the 15th century. It has an original door, framed with helmets, with a shield up by two men of primitive design; inside there is a Gothic courtyard classical in design, a graceful staircase and painted ceilings. It is now a residence hall for foreigners doing Summer courses and for scholarship students of the College of Fine Arts. It also houses students at the Teachers' College. It has also been greatly changed inside.

Next door we find the palace which belonged to the Uceda-Peralta family and which is today the Deputation Provincial, with a good granite façade, although it is incomplete, and an excellent windowed courtyard. It houses several works of art of merit.

View of the façade of the Casa de las Cadenas (House of chains).

Romanic door of the Palace of the Marquis of Lozoya.

View of the courtyard of the Palace of the Marquis of Ar

HOUSES WITH TOWERS

Many other towers, in perennial dialogue with the church spires, are silhouetted against the sky, towering above the city, warlike and militant, recalling the distant past when their mission was to watch and defend the city. The ones that catch our eye are Arias-Davila, Lozoya, Hercules, Diego de Rueda, etc. The first one belongs to the Diego Arias-Davila palace, built in the 15th century, with beautiful graphite work on it bringing out the two colours of the stone. It slim outline, broken by the merlons and machicolation gallery, rises up, continuously on parade, over the Plaza de los Huertos. The palace, which was much battered in the past, was restored a few years ago and is now used by the local Taxation Board. There are still one or two caissoned ceilings to be seen.

The graceful turret of the Lozoya, built in the 14th century lords over the spectacular scene of the lovely Plaza de San Martin an arrogant reminder of historic days gone by. It was built by the Cuellar family and then went to the Aguilar family, whose coat of arms is displayed on the keystone of the door. This coat of arms also corresponded to the Marqueses of Lozoya in the 17th century. The attached palace is a noble plateresque building, with a beautiful courtyard, galleries and extensive rooms.

The Hercules tower, which forms part of the mansion which has been the Dominican convent since the 16th century, heightens the beauty of the Plaza de la Trinidad with its classical outlines. The actual structure of the tower could be attributed to the 15th century, although paintings found in some of the chambers denote an earlier origin, possibly the 12th century.

At the foot of the staircase there is a granite sculpture, of Roman filiation, which represents Hercules astride on the head of a boar. The outside walls of this great mansion come convent appear to be even older than the Romanic walls and some critics have been led to suppose that they were built during the last few years of the Roman occupation of Segovia.

The tower of the house of Diego de Rueda, situated in the typical street called Calle de Escuderos, is artistically inferior to the ones mentioned above. However, in the ruins of this palace which belonged to the afore-mentioned governor, there is a 15th century Gothic courtyard, which gives the impression of strong character with its high fusts, old wooden galleries, carved windows and the solemn patina of the centuries in its dramatic stones; it is a very exceptional courtyard which undoubtedly is worth restoring and fortunately, it seems that this will be done, thus saving it from complete ruin.

The other houses with towers are the Casa de Chinchon, in the calle de Juan Bravo, which has an interesting courtyard, restored some years ago, and the Casa de Segovia, which has already been mentioned.

Tower of the Arias-Davila palace.

Hercules tower and façade of the Dominican church.

Tower of the Lozoya palace. ⟶

OTHER IMPORTANT BUILDINGS

The Casa Consistorial, the Town Hall, is situated in the Plaza de Franco - Plaza Mayor. It was built during the first decades of the 17th century, in accordance with plans drawn up by Pedro de Brizuela. Its style is a type of Renaissance known as «Casa de Austria». It houses the various departments of the Borough Council, the session hall, the mayor's parlour, etc. There is also a sumptuous room, called the «Sala Blanca» (White room), in the Isabeline style, and some valuable works of art, such as a tryptych by Benson, two portraits by Madrazo, an alabaster relief and other paintings by various authors.

In front of the Cathedral, in the Calle del Marques del Arco, there is a palace of the same name, built during the second half of the 16th century in the Renaissance style; its very severe granite façade is adorned with grilles and classical wrought iron balconies. Behind the aristocratic vestibule, there is a very lovely renaissance courtyard, with windowed galleries, decorated with medallions, gargoyles and exquisite carving. It is undoubtedly the best courtyard in Segovia. The palace, which belonged to Cardinal Espinosa who died in 1572, contains some richly decorated rooms and some valuable works of art.

The famous Casa de los Picos, situated in the Calle de Juan Bravo, is greatly admired for its original façade on which each ashlar is finished off in a diamond shaped point, with its impressive entrance and La Hoz family coat of arms above the door. Inside there is an interesting windowed courtyard, with a socle of Talavera ceramic. The façade would appear to have been built at the end of the 15th century. The magnificent entrance in the city wall, known as the San Martin gateway and demolished by the Town Council in 1883, was situated right where this façade ends.

In the square named after the Queen, Doña Juana, who was Enrique IV's second wife, there is an old mansion, with a more modern vestibule and courtyard, with two interesting Moorish doors from what was in the 15th century the palace of Enrique IV, copies of which —as we have already mentioned— can be seen in the King's Bedroom in the castle. There are some caissoned ceiling's on the top floors of this mansion.

The Bishop's Palace, situated in the Plaza de San Esteban, extends its granite façade, of cushioned ashlars, down the whole length of the square. It was built towards the end of the 16th century and was restored and extended in the 18th century. It has a wide courtyard of the later period and large well decorated and furnished rooms.

Other important palaces are the Juan Cascales palace, now the Public Works Department, in the Plaza de Oquendo, and the old building of the Alhondiga, both built in the 15th century.

Corner of the courtyard in the Casa de Diego de Rueda.

Façade and courtyard of the Episcopal palace

Entrance to the old Public Granary,
now the Municipal Archives.

Façade of the Casa de Juan de Cascales. ——

PROVINCIAL MUSEUM AND HISTORICAL ARCHIVES

In the Calle de San Agustin, in front of the «18 de julio» building, there is an old mansion, with obvious 15th century characteristics, which is an interesting example. It has a lovely main entrance, a typical vestibule and a medieval style courtyard; some of the rooms are also very ancient. This house, which has been named «Casa del Hidalgo» or «Squire's House», is now the Provincial Museum for paintings, sculptures and engravings. Also part of this house is the Gothic chapel, which at one time was the Old People's Hospital —close to the Plaza de San Martin— which now houses mainly prehistoric findings and objects founding in Visigoth settlements in the province.

The Provincial Museum has on show a rich collection of paintings, carvings and engravings, mostly from no longer existing curches and convents. Although the collection is not exceptional, the are several items worthy of note, especially several 15th and 16th century Hispano-Flemish tablets, including a tryptych called «Master of the carnations»; the Contreras tablet; an Adoration of the Kings from the Berruguete workshop and other works of different schools and periods, which are all tastefully displayed. There are some engravings by Durero and Rembrandt which are also worthy of mention.

The former Royal Prison is situated in the Calle de Juan Bravo, close to the church os San Martin; it underwent various reforms in the 16th and 17th century, the last one carried out by Jose del Ris, the architect, being especially important. Te building, which was fitted out as a provincial prison, was used as such until 1933 when the prison was transferred to another part of the city. Lope de Vega was held prisoner here in 1577.

In 1946 the building was adapted to take the Historical archives and the Provincial Library. Two rooms in the ground floor were also fitted out as exhibition halls, one of which has a lovely Romanic entrance which came from an abandoned hermitage close to Segovia. The building still preserves a small curiously constructed chapel and also the outer entrance to the building which was done in 1631 by Pedro de Brizuela.

In the Archives there are several important documents on Segovia's past. With regard to the Provincial Library, it runs an excellent daily function.

Provincial Museum. Reliefs from the Santa Columba altarpiece (16th c.) and Descent from the Cross by Clerigo Contreras, a 15th-16th c. tablet.

Façade of the former Old People's chapel, next door to the Provincial Museum and façade of the old prison (17th c.).

A SUPERB CORNER OF THE CITY

In between the church of San Martin and the row of houses with the Lozoya tower, there was a strip of land on a slope which the City Council decided to put in order in about the middle of the last century. The work was carried out by the municipal architect of the time, Antonio Vazquez de Zuñiga and he was able to create one of the most beautiful public spots to be seen. However, in 1921, the fountain, which used to stand where the statue of Juan Bravo is today, was removed thus impairing the character of this beautiful setting by altering the perspective, which was not a very fortunate step taken by the City Council.

Two squares —Medina del Campo and San Martin— make up this extraordinary setting, joined by a succession of steps which have been well planned and constructed, thus giving the spot a spectacular aspect. The lower part of the first house on the right, with its Plateresque doorway, belonged to the Segovian doctor and writer Jeronimo de Alcala, the author of the famous novel «The Gifted Talker, or Alonso, the lad with many masters», who died in 1632. Further on there is another characteristic building, with a granite door and excellent graphite work. These two houses and the circular platform make up the small square of Medina del Campo.

On a higher level, we continue with the Lozoya Tower, which we have already mentioned, and next door, another lovely house with a doorway, an angle window and a very fitting gallery. Next door, we come to what was Solier's houses, a nobly porportioned building, with a lovely Plateresque gallery, which has been walled in, and a façade of great artistic interest. The square is shut off at the back by another nobly designed mansion which has an excellent doorway, coats of arms and a small tower. Close to this building we have what was the Gothic chapel attached to the Old People's Hospital and which is today attached to the Provincial Museum. At the entrance to this chapel there are two granite figures of Celtiberian origina, which are representative of the culture of the «Verracos».

The left side of this splendid square is taken up by the church of San Martin and looking from the higher level towards the back of the lower part, we find the lovely 15th century Gothic façade of the house which once belonged to the Tordesillas family, with a doorway framed with al-ifriz and a beautiful gallery.

For some years now there has been a project for transferring the statue to some other spot and reinstating the fountain in its original situation.

A beautiful view of the Plaza de San Martin. ⟶

Church of San Martin.

Façade of the Casa de Tordesillas, called Juan Bravo's house. ⟶

THE ERESMA VALLEY

On previous pages we have already mentioned the valley of the river Eresma, a landscape of orchards and poplar groves, stretching out to the north of the city. This valley is of marked interest to the history of Segovia, as it still contains many reminders of the past, starting with the rock caves in which prehistoric remains have been discovered. As we have already said, the picturesque district of San Lorenzo is situated in this valley. The convent of the Bernadine nuns of St. Vincent is the oldest in Segovia; the Parral monastery; the convent of the Carmelitas Descalzos Order and the ruins of the churches of San Blas and San Gil.

What was the Mint until 1869 and now converted into a flour mill still stands on the banks of the river. It was founded by Philip II in 1583 and built to the plans of Herrera. The Spanish monarch employed the best coiners in Europe here and the very best coins of the period and for some time after were minted here. It was abandoned in 1869 and sold as National Property, after having been used for various purposes; it is now a flour mill. A few years ago a fire destroyed part of the building and was restored but also modified.

And where the river changes its course to leave behind the city boundaries, the Sanctuary of the Virgin of the Fuencisla, Patron of Segovia and its Land, a place fervently attended by the Segovians, is situated under the stern bulk of the «Peñas Grajeras». A poplar grove stretches out in front of the Sanctuary and water from thousands of springs runs down between the rocks. The primitive 13th century sanctuary was built on the very spot where the miracle of Maria del Salto occurred, the Jewess who was thrown from the rocks. The original building was replaced by the present one which was built towards the end of the 16th century and beginning of the 17th century according to plans designed by Francisco de Mora. It is in the shape of a Latin cross and has a splendid altarpiece at the high altar, done by Pedro de la Torre and with paintings by Francisco Camilo, topped by a hardly visible picture by Ribera. The grille is of interest as it was guilded at the expense of the carding and wool combing industries in the 18th century. The beautiful Baroque style sacristy is also worthy of note. The Virgin's treasures are also very valuable, both in clothes as well as in jewelry given by the people of Segovia over the centuries. The crown is of special interest as it was financed through popular subscription and it was used for canonically crowning the Virgin in 1916.

Former Mint, in the Eresma Valley, founded by Philip II.

Altarpiece and statue of the Virgin of Fuencisla.

Sanctuary of Fuencisla, under the «Peñas Grajeras».

La Granja de San Ildefonso. Gardens and Palace.

THE JEWISH QUARTERS

A narrow street, which still preserves its ancient name of «Calle de la Judería Vieja», starts from the Plaza del Corpus, where the façade of the convent which from the 13th to the 15th century was a Hebrew Synagogue, as already mentioned, is situated. Another analogous street continues, once called Calle del Sol, in which the house where Dr. Laguna lived is situated, and the Calle de Santa Ana branches off to the left down steps, with an archaic air. In the last house in this street there is a niche with a statue of Santa Ana, who is the patron of the cobblers. Through a small deserted alley we come out into another narrow lane which branches out into the Calle de Martínez Campos, once known as «La Mala Bajada». The needles and battlements of the Cathedral rise up to the right and on the left we come to the roughened face of the wall.

The street goes down sharply, going through a tunnel, which was constructed little more than twenty years ago with obvious damage to the wall, and finally comes out into the Plaza del Socorro, on to which the San Andrés gateway opens. It is still the heart of the old Jewish Quarter, in spite of the reforms to which it has been subjected and is undoubtedly seeped in antiquity, calling to mind long lost pages in history and remote lives.

On the other side of the Plaza del Socorro, a street by the name of «Calle de la Judería Nueva» begins its climb upwards; it is graded in steps, flanked by buildings of humble design, giving this street a genuine air and gives us a good example of what was the warp of the Jewish synagogue in times gone by. Where the street bends round, a house still stands, with ancient architectonic remains, where legend states that the Jewish doctor Don Mayr lived. He was the protagonist in the supernatural occurrence of the «Miracle in the Synagogue» in 1410.

If we go down the calle del Socorro, the one following after the previous one, we come to some ancient dies in the walls, which at one time sheltered the palace of the Condes del Sol, later a convent for the Order of Carmelitas calzados and which have been used from the 17th century for the municipal slaughter house. The castle rises up in front and a long way below, the stream Clamores runs in the hollow. This stream has been recently covered over all along its course until it comes out into the river Eresma at the foot of the castle. On the opposite slope above the bed of the stream, there is a pine forest covering the ground which was once a Jewish cemetery, where tombs have been discovered on various occasions.

Calle de Santa Ana. →

Segovia covered in Snow, from the Cathedral tower.

Calle de la Juderia Nueva. ⟶

SOME OTHER INTERESTING CORNERS

We have mentioned so far in this book characteristic squares, streets and corners. Now, without wishing to overdo the subject, we are going to deal with other corners of the city which have a genuine air and undoubtable vintage.

The Plaza de Franco —Plaza Mayor or just «La Plaza»— is an obviously impressive square. It is surrounded by porticoes on three of its side and the west flank is closed off by the magnificent symphony of the Cathedral apse. For many centuries this square was the city's market, a meeting place and a place for popular festivities.

The Plaza de la Merced, for the most part, covers the site of the monastery of the Mercederian Order, and is also incorporated into a large garden, with a circular fountain, and another smaller square presided over by the church of San Andres. In front of the square, the Convent founded by St. Teresa rears up behind its sombre walls.

The Plaza de los Espejos (mirrors) is another typical square, in which the granite façade of a 15th century house, with its doorway and other buildings, seeped in antiquity, stand out. The square takes its name from the mirrors which Enrique IV's palace had on the frontage looking onto this sector.

A rather smaller square is the Plaza de Avendaño, where the Aqueduct ends. It is very much enhanced by a lovely house with a Romanic doorway and good balconies. The walls of a convent line one side of this square and the last bricked-in arch of the Aqueduct can also be seen there.

The Plaza de Colmenares, on the northern sector of the wall, is a spot full of memories with lovely gardens enhancing the church of San Juan de los Caballeros and the mansion which belonged to Rodrigo de Contreras. This spot is shortly to undergo major reforms.

The street Calle del Grabador Espinosa begins close to the Plaza de los Espejos. It is a steep street with steps, with an air of antiquity, in which there is a typical small yard, seeped in history. Ancient houses of distant origin loom up either side of the street. It comes out into the narrow street called Calle del Sauco, what has a down-at-heel look about it.

The Calle de los Desamparados joins the Calle de Daoiz and Covarrubias, in the San Esteban district. It is narrow and steep. The street contains the Convent of San Juan de Dios and the little house where the poet Antonio Machado lived for twelve years. There is also a stone bust of the poet on view.

The beautiful Paseo del Salon stretches out on the lee of the wall. There is a lovely view towards the south and the spot is a favourite with the very old and the very young.

Partial view of the Plaza Mayor, with the Town Hall and Cathedral.

Calle de los Desamparados.

Busto of A. Machado in the house where he lived,
in the calle de los Desamparados.

PRESENT DAY SEGOVIA

As a result of a long decadent process which began with the 17th century, Segovia commenced this century with a population of scarcely more than 14,000 inhabitants. The last remains of the flourishing industries of past centuries had been extinguished. The livelihood of the citizens became an essentially family affair, where even the most tedious of events acquired unusual importance.

Even at the end of the second decade of this century, the inhabitants of Segovia scarcely amounted to 16,000. However, some important industries were created and life began to acquire a more decided course, although the rythm was slow. It was during the years following the Civil War that the city began to move forwards, spreading out beyond its ancient boundaries. The number of inhabitants began to increase notably —in 1940 there were more than 25,000 registered inhabitants and now there are almost 40,000.

As from 1940 a gradual building process began to move out towards the east and south of the city, following the same urban expansion routes as in the 15th and 16th centuries, when Segovia had more than 60,000 inhabitants. In the very places where suburbs had once existed before the decadence, new populous districts have risen up under the names of El Carmen and San José. In the same way the district of San Lorenzo has been considerably expanded and so have areas south east of Segovia, known as Las Lastras. Within the city itself, new buildings are rapidly going up in the districts of El Mercado and San Millan, transforming these ancient corners into crowded hives, even though in some instances the historical and monumental character of Segovia may have been damaged by unsuitable buildings within the walled-in area.

Industry and Commerce have developed at the same speed up to a point that the exclusive agricultural activities of the past can no longer take first place. Today Segovia has lost a great deal of agricultural importance and industry, which in the past had been essential to its livelihood. This goes to show that Segovia is growing and developing from every point of view.

Among the important buildings constructed over the last few years, we pick out the Civil Government Offices, in the Plaza del Seminario; the Law Courts, in the Calle de San Agustin, and the magnificent building of the Caja de Ahorros (Savings Bank) in the Avenida de Fernandez Ladreda.

Paseo Ezequiel Gonzalez.

Roast suckling pig or Toston: the typical dish in Segovia
at the Meson de Candido.

THE PROVINCE
THE CASTLE ROUTES (I)

If we leave Segovia by the Madrid-Leon road, we turn off at the 8 km. post to Turegano, which is sone 34 kms. from the capital. The very typical square of this town, with the castle looming above it, is known throughout the world. The castle is a 15th century construction, built by the bishop, Juan Arias Davila, and surrounds a 13th century Romanic church dedicated to San Miguel. Around the castle there are the remains of a probably 12th century wall, which must have belonged to a previous fortress. Antonio Perez, Philip II's secretary, was held prisoner in this castle. The church of Santiago is worthy of note and there are also some interesting typical buildings.

Sepulveda, which is situated on a high rise in the ground, around which the reivers Caslilla and Duraton flow, is like an altarpiece carved in stone. The Romanic church of El Salvador, built at the end of the 11th century, stands out on the crest of the hill, with its graceful outlines. The church of the Virgen de la Peña, the patron saint of Sepulveda, looks out over the River Duraton. It is Romanic in style and most interesting to visit. Ruins of the ancient castle and its walls still stand in the square, some of its doors still intact. There are many blazoned houses with fine façades in Sepulveda; also stout strong buildings and typical corners which give this town an unusual air and a feeling of importance.

The castle of Castilnovo, once owned by Don Alvaro de Luna and now the property of the Marqueses de Quintanar, is situated 8 kms. from Sepulveda in the middle of a lovely park. Its present structure is 15th century although it was built on top of an older castle. There is a church attached with a high tower, and inside the castle, which is periodically inhabited, there are some lovely well decorated and furnished rooms. The castle has been recently restored with undoubtable success and makes a lovely picture, with an aura of history about it.

About 16 kms. from this town, the town of Pedraza, surrounded by a wall with only one entrance, and situated on a high rock, is outlined spectacularly against the sky, presided over by the Romanic church of San Juan. The main square is famous with its typical porticoes and fine mansions, which ornaments the marvel of the «Council's big elm». The 15th century castle, built by Constable Pedro Fernandez de Velasco, is now in ruins, except for the turret which was used as a studio by the painter Ignacio Zuloaga, who acquired it in 1928. The castle is perched on the top of the rock on which Pedraza is situated, overlooking a picturesque valley of orchards and trees, with magnificent views.

Castilnovo.

Square and castle at Turegano.

Castle and square of the lovely town of Pedraza.

A lovely corner in Sepulveda.

Cuellar. Castle, Mudejar apse and tombs in the church
of San Esteban.

THE CASTLE ROUTES (II)

The road from Segovia to Coca passes through Santa Maria de Nieva, a town founded at the end of the 14th century, in which there is a very beautiful Gothic church to be admired. It has a cloister of the Romanic transitional period, which is really remarkable, with exquisitely carved capitals. The church also contains a very interesting altarpiece attributed to Berruguete.

Santa Maria is seventeen kilometers away from Coca. The road runs through one of the most prosperous towns in the province: Nava de la Asuncion, which has a wealth of wood industries and by-products, as is to be expected of a land covered in pine forests. Coca —the Celtiberian Cauca, the home of Teodosio the Great— is situated between the rivers Eresma and Voltoya which surround the castle. There are the remains of the ancient wall, with a Mudejar style door. The Gothic style parish church is worthy of note as it contains the tombs of the Fonseca family, the lords of Coca, some of which were carved by Bartolome Ordoñez.

The Moorish style castle, which was built in the 15th century, was one of the most sumptuous constructions of its type, on account of the wealth and splendour of its elements, making it comparable, in some ways with the Alhambra in Granada, as it has suffered outrages and ransacking causing the castle serious damage. It has been restored by the Ministry of Agriculture for establishing a school for Forestry Commissioners. The exterior of the castle once more stands in all its former glory.

There are 29 kilometers from Coca to Cuellar, via Chañe. The latter town, which is the most populous in the province after the capital, has a 15th century Gothic castle, which belonged to the Duke of Alburquerque and was extended in the 16th century. For some years it was used as a prison, but it has now been relieved from that duty. It is a stoutly constructed building, very much in tone with the tastes of the period in which it was erected. It has been restored on several occasions, but still preserves a defined character. It has a lovely Plateresque courtyard and beautiful galleries. Espronceda was held prisoner there.

Cuellar, formely the Celtiberian Colenda, preserves some valuable monuments from the past, especially the churches of San Martin, San Andres and San Esteban, with some very suggestive and expressive Romanic brick apses. There are also remains of the old wall and the Hospital and some of the church towers are important too.

The return to Segovia can be done through Carbonero el Mayor, a flourishing town, with an excellent Gothic church which has a Plateresque altarpiece and valuable paintings.

Coca. View of the Castle. —

— La Granja de San Ildefonso. Palace façade.

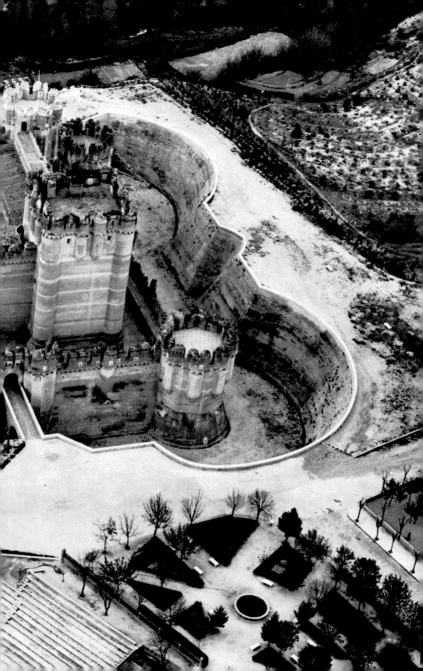

Santa Maria de Nieva. St. Jerome, carved in the style of
Berruguete and capitals in the cloister

←— Aerial view of Coca castle.

ROYAL PALACES — SAN ILDEFONSO

Te grounds now covered by the Royal Estate of San Ilde-fonso were used in the distant past by the Kings of Castile for hunting. This was especially so of Enrique IV who had a hermitage built dedicated to San Ildefonso in order to be able to fulfill his religious duties. Years later, the Catholic Kings donated the hermitage to the Jerome monks of El Parral, who built around it a convalescent and rest home, or «granja». This is why the names San Ildefonso and La Granja originated.

During the second decade of the 18th century, Philip V, who was very much taken with the beauty of the place, thought up the project of building a palace. This was begun in 1721, in accordance with plans drawn up by Teodoro Ardemans. The work was carried out so fast that the project was finished two years later. The gardens were laid out at the same time in accordance with the style imposed on by Le Notre at Versaille. This work was done by Boutelou and Carlier and the monumental fountains, statues and ornamental details of the gardens were carried out by Demandre, Thierri, Fremin and Pitue. The Collegiate church was also built at the same time. This was where Philip V and Isabel de Farnesio were to be buried. The church also has paintings by Maella and Bayeu.

The palace is now a most interesting museum on account of the artistic wealth on view inside, both of tapestries, paintings, furniture, lamps, etc. as well as of the very magnificence of the chambers and rooms. The extraordinary collection of tapestries is perhaps the best in Europe. The palace and its rooms can all be visited.

With regard to the gardens, we only need say that they are situated in one of the most beautiful landscapes. This beauty is enhanced by the impressive nearness of the Guadarrama mountains which surround the palace with their high peaks. Fountains, statues, urns, cascades and other ornamental details follow on from each other in complete harmony and good taste along the whole length and breadth of the gardens. You should especially note the fountains of Andromeda, Carrera de Caballos, (horse race), Baños de Diana (Diana's Baths), la Fama, Canastillo and the great cascade. The long lake, known as «El Mar» (the sea) stretches out on a higher level, supplying water to all the fountains. The leafy woods which populate these splendid gardens are full of variety and magnificence. San Ildefonso is situated some eleven kilometers from Segovia, on the Madrid-Leon road.

La Granja de San Ildefonso. Gardens in the Royal Palace.

Tapestry room and Neptune fountain at the Royal Palace.

As we leave San Ildefonso, there is a road which branches off to the left, close to the Segovia bridge, which after passing close to the boundaries of the Robledo Military Camp, joins up with the San Rafael road. The road which leads to the Palace of Riofrio, now very close by, begins after the village of Revenga, close to what was the church of Cepones and which is now a dwelling.

This neoclassical palace, situated in the middle of a large holm oak forest, was built by Isabel de Farnesio, after the death of Philip V, although it was finished during the reign of Charles III. The estate which crosses the Riofrio stream, later extended with land bought from other landowners, was acquired from the Marquis of Paredes for the construction of this palace. Work began in 1752, in accordance with the plans of the architect Rabaglio and was finished ten years later, although some aspects which had been planned for in the beginning were not carried out.

The forest surrounding the palace and covering some 700 hectares of land —populated by deer, buck and stags— was the scene of many magnificent hunts during the reigns of Alfonso XII and Alfonso XIII. Over the last few years many of the above mentioned animals have been taken from Riofrio to other Spanish parks and forests.

The palace was recently restored and there is now a very important museum which, as in the case of San Ildefonso, houses very good collections of paintings, furniture, tapestries, etc. The palace courtyard is very splendid and the main staircase is magnificent with its daringly original and elegantly designed sweep.

The beauty of landscape surrounding the Riofrio palace and the artistic wealth exhibited in the magnificent rooms, have recently made it a very popular tourist attraction. After viewing the art treasures, visitors have the chance of relaxing in the lovely forests of holm oaks and other species, in which the deer wander grazing right up to the edge of the road.

At present the Hunting Museum is being installed in the palace and will be opened very shortly to the public. Riofrio is situated some seven kilometers from Segovia, right beneath the Guadarrama mountains.

View of the façade of the Riofrio palace.

OTHER INTERESTING PLACES

If we leave Segovia by the Soria-Plasencia road, which runs parallel to the Guadarrama mountains, we go past the mountain village 'of Navafria. There is here the best planted pine forest in Spain, furrowed by many streams all containing exquisite trout. Further on we come to the town of Pradena, a very typical hamlet, with a rather ornate 18th century neoclassical church. The most interesting part of this town is a large cave discovered a few years ago, which is famous for the beauty of its colouring.

The town of Riaza, which is the burrough headquarters, has been concerned for many centuries with industrial and agricultural activities. The town itself is pleasantly typical, the mountain style of architecture blending in well with the new modern constructions. The renaissance style parish church is interesting and the Sanctuary of the Virgin of Hontares is not far away.

Ayllon, once owned by Don Alvaro de Luna, some twenty kilometers from Riaza, still preserves the remains of the medieval castle, as well as the convent founded by St. Francis of Assisi. The town square, which was restored not long ago, is of special interest. There is still a door in the old wall and close by stands the lovely Gothic façade of what was the Contreras palace, which has many impressive rooms.

Maderuelo, an ancient fortress town built on the river Riaza, still retains its medieval character, a reminder of past splendours. At the foot of the town, close to the river itself, we find the hermitage of the Templarians, which once had an extraordinary set of Romanic paintings, now exhibited in the Prado Museum in Madrid. The Maderuelo church is interesting.

Fuentidueña, a town in the north of the province, is connected with Alfonso VIII who lived there on occasions. The special characteristics of the town are the 12th century walls and the magnificent church of San Miguel, as was also the church of San Martin, now in ruins, whose superb Romanic apse is now in the New York Museum. Fuentidueña has other vestiges of the past to show, thus proving its ancient aristocratic lineage.

Villacastin, thirty kilometers from Segovia in the direction of Avila, has a magnificent church, with certain Gothic elements. It was restorer by Fr. Antonio de Villacastin at the end of the 16th century in the Renaissance style. The mountain town of El Espinar also has a splendid renaissance church, with a magnificent altarpiece and interesting works of art.

140

Riaza. Tower of the Parish Church. ⟶

Partial view of Fuentidueña and Ayllon town square.

Villacastin. Parish church (16th c.) and National Highway Inn.

The harrow and the pasture, two constant elements in the
economy of Segovia.

INFORMACION PRACTICA SEGOVIA

La mayor parte de estos datos, han sido facilitados por la
Delegación Provincial de Información y Turismo de Segovia. Información puesta al día el 3-2-72.

INFORMATION PRATIQUE SEGOVIE

*La plupart de ces données ont été fournies par la Délégation
Provinciale d'Information et Tourisme. Information mise à
jour le 3-2-1972*

PRACTICAL INFORMATION SEGOVIA

The marjority of this information has been suplied by the
Provincial Delegation of Information and Tourism. This
leaflet was brought up to date as at 3rd February 1972

Entre las provincias que rodean a Madrid, Segovia es la más septentrional. Ocupa una extensión de 7.000 Km² y tiene 210.000 habitantes. El clima es continental, con veranos frescos y agradables. Es una provincia fundamentalmente agrícola y ganadera. El cultivo de cereales y la cría de ganado ovino y vacuno son las fuentes principales de riqueza.

Pedraza, Cuéllar, Sepúlveda, Riaza, Santa María la Real de Nieva y Coca son las poblaciones más importantes desde los puntos de vista administrativo, histórico y monumental. Mención aparte merece La Granja de San Ildefonso, famosa tanto por la belleza de su palacio neoclásico y los jardines que la rodean como por la tradicional artesanía del cristal. La región que se extiende a los pies de la Cordillera Central es una prestigiosa zona de verano.

La cocina segoviana tiene en el cochinillo asado su expresión definitiva. El chorizo de Cantimpalos es uno de los más suculentos embutidos de la charcutería nacional. Segovia, la capital, se encuentra entre las ciudades más bellas de España. Su famoso acueducto romano, las múltiples iglesias románicas y la impresionante silueta del Alcázar forman un conjunto de gran atractivo.

Durante las fiestas de San Pedro, del 24 al 29 de junio, se celebran corridas de toros y manifestaciones folklóricas.

La province de Ségovie est la plus septentrionale de celles qui entourent Madrid. Elle a une superficie de 7.000 Km² et compte 210.000 habitants. Le climat, continental, a des étés frais et agréables.

C'est une province essentiellement consacrée à l'élevage. La culture des céréales et l'élevage ovin et bovin sont les principales sources de richesse.

Pedraza, Cuéllar, Sepúlveda, Riaza, Santa María la Real de Nieva et Coca sont des centres importants du point de vue administratif, historique et monumental. Une mention spéciale doit être faite de la Granja de San Ildefonso, célèbre par son palais neo-classique et les jardins qui l'entourent et son artisanat traditionnel du verre. La région située au pied de la Cordillère Centrale attire de nombreux estivants.

Le cochon de lait rôti est sans doute le meilleur plat de la cuisine ségovienne. Le «chorizo» de Cantimpalos figures parmi les charcuteries nationales les plus savoureuses.

Ségovie est une des plus belles villes d'Espagne. Le fameux aqueduc romain, les nombreuses églises romanes et l'impressionnante silhouette de l'Alcázar forment un ensemble inoubliable.

Des corridas et différentes manifestations folkloriques ont lieu du 24 ou 29 juin à l'ocasion des fêtes de San Pedro.

Segovia is the most northerly of the provinces abutting on Madrid. It has an area of 7,000 sq. Kms. and a population of 210,000 The climate is continental, but agreeably cool in summer. The province is given over in the main to agriculture and stockbreeding. The chief sources of wealth are cereals, sheep and cattle.

Administratively and historically the chief towns are Pedraza, Cuéllar, Sepúlveda, Riaza, Santa María La Real de Nieva and Coca. Particular mention should be made of La Granja de San Ildefonso, famous for its neo-classical palace and gardens, and for its traditional glassware. The foot-hills of the Cordillera Central are a popular summer resort.

The local speciality is «cochinillo asado» (roast suckling-pig). Camtimpalos sausage is one of the best types in the country.

Segovia with its famous Roman aqueduct, many Romanesque churches, and the impressive Alcázar, is one the most beautiful cities in Spain.

The annual St. Peter's Fair (24-29 June) includes bull-fights and folk festivities.

147

MONUMENTOS Y HORAS
DE VISITA

ACUEDUCTO. En el centro de la ciudad, monumento de fama mundial y una de las obras mejor conservadas del mundo.

ALCAZAR. Fortaleza-Palacio de los Reyes de Castilla, construido entre los siglos XII al XVI. Impresionante vista exterior desde la alameda de la Fuencisla.
Horas de visita:
Verano: de 10,30 a 19,30.
Invierno: de 10,30 a 18,30.
Precio de entrada: 15 pesetas (Tomavistas: 10 pesetas; cámaras: 5 pesetas).

LA CATEDRAL. Iniciada su construcción en el siglo XVI en sustitución de la anterior; por su belleza y elegancia de sus líneas se la denomina «La dama de las catedrales españolas».
Horas de visita al Claustro, Museo y Sala Capitular:
Verano: de 9 a 19 horas.
Invierno: de 9 a 13 y de 15 a 18 horas.
Festivos: de 9 a 18 horas.
Precio de entrada: 10 pesetas.

SAN MILLAN. El ejemplar más importante del románico segoviano; fue erigida en la primera mitad del siglo XII. (Fuera de las horas de culto, la llave puede solicitarse en la calle de Pelaires, núm. 1).

SAN ESTEBAN. Iglesia románica de los siglos XII y XIII, cuya torre de seis cuerpos de sillares de caliza, es denominada «Reina de las torres bizantinas».

MONASTERIO DEL PARRAL. Fue fundado por Enrique IV y el marqués de Villena en el siglo XV para la Orden Jerónima. Valioso retablo plateresco y bellos sepulcros.
Horas de visita:
Verano: de 10 a 13,30 y de 15,30 a 19,30.
Invierno: de 10 a 13,30 y de 15 a la puesta del sol.
Precio de entrada: 10 pesetas.

IGLESIA DE LA VERA CRUZ. Fundada por la Orden del Temple a comienzos del siglo XIII; su planta es un polígono de doce lados. Monumento nacional desde el año de 1909.
Horas de visita:
De 10 a 13,30 y de 16,30 hasta la puesta del sol. Cerrado los lunes. Precio de entrada: 10 pesetas; con reducción a grupo.

CARMELITAS DESCALZOS. Convento fundado por San Juan de la Cruz en 1588 en un pintoresco paraje a orillas del río Eresma; en él se guarda el sepulcro del Santo Carmelita.
Horas de visita:
De 8 a 13,30 y de 16 a 20,30 horas.

SAN ANTONIO EL REAL. Palacio de recreo de Enrique IV, convento de Franciscanos después, y ahora de monjas clarisas. Magníficos artesonados, bellos retablos y valiosos trípticos flamencos.
Horas de visita:
De 10 a 14 y de 15 a la puesta del sol.
Precio de entrada: 10 pesetas.

SAN JUSTO. Bella iglesia románica del siglo XII en la que recientemente se han descubierto magníficas pinturas murales de la misma época y otros elementos artísticos. (Fuera de las horas de culto, puede solicitarse la llave en la Plaza de San Justo, núm. 2).

SAN MARTIN. Iglesia románica que guarda valiosas obras de arte escultórico y buenas pinturas, situada junto a la bella plaza de su nombre. Destacan los magníficos capiteles de su atrio.

SAN JUAN DE LOS CABALLEROS. Iglesia románica, hoy interesante Museo de Cerámica, fundado por el genial artista Zuloaga.

LAS MURALLAS. Probablemente son tan antiguas como la ciudad misma con muchas reparaciones, como es lógico. Son típicas las puertas de «Santiago o del Refugio», «San Cebrián», «San Andrés» y «Postigo del Consuelo».

LAS CANONJIAS. Calles evocadoras, con sus típicos rincones, que vieron el paso de cortejos reales y el fausto de ceremonias religiosas en los días de la vieja catedral de Santa María, a partir de 1147; hoy espléndido conjunto urbano.

SANTA CRUZ LA REAL. Fue la primera fundación en nuestra Patria de Santo Domingo de Guzmán, en 1217, siendo la iglesia actual magnífica muestra del estilo gótico, obra de los Reyes Católicos. En el interior se conserva la «Cueva de Santo Domingo».

PALACIO DEL MARQUES DE LOZOYA. Construido en el siglo XIII, conserva una bella portada románica, si bien el palacio fue restaurado en el siglo XV.

PALACIO DEL MARQUES DEL ARCO. Renacimiento español de la segunda mitad del siglo XVI. Tiene un precioso patio y zaguán.

PALACIO EPISCOPAL. Comenzado a construir en la segunda mitad del siglo XVI, concluyéndose en el XVIII por el Obispo de Segovia, Doctor Murillo.

CASA DE LOS PICOS. Original edificio segoviano. Hasta finales del siglo pasado tuvo adosada la puerta de la muralla denominada de «San Martín».

TORREON DE ARIAS DAVILA. Construido en el siglo XV, frente al entonces palacio del Monarca Enrique IV. Es de destacar su esgrafiado y esbeltez de líneas.

TORREON DE LOZOYA. Se alza en uno de los más destacados conjuntos urbanos de la ciudad, plaza de San Martín.

CASA DE JUAN CASCALES. Edificada en el siglo XV, tiene preciosos ajimeces de pizarra y antiguo esgrafiado. Forma parte de un bello rincón en el centro de la ciudad.

MONUMENTS ET HEURES DE VISITE

AQUEDUC. Au centre de la ville, monument de réputation mondiale, une des oeuvres romaines les mieux conservées du monde.

ALCAZAR. Forteresse-Palais des Rois de Castille, construit entre les XIIe et XVIe ss. Impressionnante vue extérieure, depuis l'alameda de la Fuencisla.
Heures de visite:
Eté: de 10.30 à 19.30.
Hiver: de 10.30 à 18.30.
Prix d'entrée: 15 ptas. caméras: 10 ptas. appareils photographiques: 5 ptas.

CATHEDRALE. Sa construction fut commencée au XVIe s. en remplacement de l'antérieur; en raison de la beauté et de l'élégance de ses lignes, on l'appelle «la dame des cathédrales espagnoles».
Heures de visite au Cloître, Musée et Salle Capitulaire:
Eté: de 9 à 19 heures.
Hiver: de 9 à 13 et de 15 à 18.
Jours fériés: de 9 à 18.
Prix: 10 ptas.

SAN MILLAN. L'exemplaire le plus important du roman ségovien, érigé à la première moitié du XIIe s. (hors des heures de culte, on peut demander la clé à la rue de Pelaires, n.o 1).

SAN ESTEBAN. Eglise romane, des XIIe et XIIIe ss, dont la tour de six corps en pierres de taille calcaire est appelée «Reine des tours byzantines».

MONASTERIO DEL PARRAL. Fondé par Henri IV et le marquis de Villena au XVe s. pour l'Ordre de Saint Jérôme. Retable platéresque précieux et beaux sépulcres.
Heures de visite:
Eté: de 10 à 13,30 et de 15,30 à 19,30.
Hiver: de 10 à 13.30 et de 15 au coucher du soleil.
Prix d'entrée: 10 ptas.

EGLISE DE LA VERA CRUZ. Fondée par l'Ordre du Temple au début du XIIIe s. Son plan est un polygone de douze côtés. Monument national depuis l'an 1909.
Heures de visite:
De 10.30 à 13.30 et de 16.30 au coucher du soleil. Fermée les lundis.
Prix d'entrée: 10 ptas. reduction pour groupes.

CARMELITES DECHAUX. Couvent fondé par St. Jean de la Croix en 1588 dans un endroit pittoresque au bord du ruisseau Eresma. On y garde le sépulcre du Saint Carmélite.
Heures de visite:
De 8 à 13.30 et de 16 à 20.30.

SAN ANTONIO EL REAL. Palais de vacances d'Henri IV, couvent de Franciscains ensuite et maintenant, de religieuses Clarisses. Magnifiques lambrissages, beaux retables et précieux triptyques flamands.
Heures de visite:
De 10 à 14 et de 15 au coucher de soleil.
Prix d'entrée: 10 ptas.

SAN JUSTO. Belle église romane du XIIe s. dans laquelle, récement, on a découvert de magnifiques peintures murales de la même époque et d'autres éléments artistiques (hors des heures de culte, on peut demander la clé à la Place de San Justo n.o 2).

SAN MARTIN. Eglise romane qui conserve de précieuses oeuvres d'art sculptural et de bonnes peintures. Elle est située près de la place du même nom. A noter les magnifiques chapiteaux de son atrium.

SAN JUAN DE LOS CABALLEROS. Eglise romane, aujourd'hui intéressant musée de céramique, fondé par le génial artiste Zuloaga.

LES MURAILLES. Sont probablement aussi anciennes que la ville même, avec beaucoup de réparations, comme c'est logique. Les portes «Santiago ou del Refugio», «San Cebriám», «San Andrés» et «Postigo del Consuelo» sont typiques.

LAS CANONJIAS. Rues évocatrices avec leurs coins typiques qui virent le passage de cortèges royaux et le faste de cérémonies religieuses aux jours de la vieille cathédrale de Santa María, à partir de 1147. Aujourd'hui, splendide ensemble urbain.

SANTA CRUZ LA REAL. Fut la première fondation dans notre Patrie de Saint Domingo de Guzmán, en 1217, et l'église actuelle est un magnifique échantillon du style gothique, oeuvre des Rois Catholiques. A l'intérieur, on conserve «La Cueva de Santo Domingo».

PALAIS DU MARQUIS DE LOZOYA. Construit au XIIIe s. conserve un beau portique roman, bien que le palais ait été restauré au XVe s.

PALAIS DU MARQUIS DEL ARCO. Renaissance espagnole de la deuxième moitié du XVIe s. Possède un beau patio et un élégant vestibule.

PALAIS EPISCOPAL. Commencé à la deuxième moitié du XVIe s. et termine au XVIIIe par l'Evêque de Ségovie, Docteur Murillo.

CASA DE LOS PICOS. Original édifice ségovien. Jusqu'à la fin du siècle passé il fut adossé à la porte de la muraille dénommée de «San Martim».

TORREON DE ARIAS DAVILA. Construit au XVe s. en face de ce qui était alors le palais du Monarque Henri IV. Il faut noter ses dessins et sa sveltesse de lignes.

TORREON DE LOZOYA. S'élève sur l'un des ensembles urbains les plus remarquables de la ville place de San Martin.

CASA DE JUAN CASCALES. Edifiée au XVe s., possède de charmantes fenêtres géminées d'ardoise et un dessin ancien. Fait partie d'un beau coin au centre de la ville.

MONUMENTS AND VISITING HOURS

AQUEDUCT. In the centre of the city, a monument of world fame and one of the best Roman works still standing in the world.

ALCAZAR. Fortress-Palace of the King's of Castile, built between the 12th and 16th centuries. Impressive view from outside from the poplar grove of Fuencisla.
Visiting hours:
Summer: 10.30 to 7.30 p. m.
Winter: 10.30 to 6.30 p. m.
Entrance fee: 15 ptas. (Cine camera: 10 ptas. and camara: 5 ptas.).

CATHEDRAL. Construction commenced in the 16th century, replacing the fomer Cathedral. It is known as the «Queen of all Spanish Cathedrals» on account of its beauty and the elegance of its outlines.
Visiting hours to the Cloister, Museum and Capitular Chamber:
Summer from 9 a. m. to 7 p. m.
Winter from 9 a. m. to 1 p. m. and from 3 p. m. to 6 p. m.
Holidays from 9 a. m. to 6 p. m.
Entrance fee: 10 ptas.

SAN MILLAN. The most important example of Segovian Romanic architecture. It was built during the second half of the 12th century. (Outside hours of worhsip, the key may be requested at no. 1 in the calle de Pelaires).

SAN ESTEBAN. 12th and 13th century Romanic church, whose six storey tower of limestone ashlars is known as «The Queen of the Bizantine towers».

EL PARRAL MONASTERY. Founded by Henry IV and the Marquis of Villena in the 15th century fot the Jerome Order. Valuable plateresque altarpiece and beautiful tombs.
Visiting hours:
Summer from 10 to 1.30 p. m. and from 3.30 p. m. to 7.30 p. m.
Winter from 10 to 1.30 p. m. and from 3 p. m. to sunset.
Entrance fee: 10 ptas.

CHURCH OF VERA CRUZ. Founded by the Order of the Temple at the beginning of the 13th century. Is in the shape of a 12 sided polygon. It has been a national monument since 1909.
Visiting hours:
From 10.30 a. m. to 1.30 p. m. and from 4.30 p. m. to sunset. Closed on Mondays.
Entrance fee: 10 ptas, with reduction for groups.

CARMELITAS DESCALZOS. Convent founded by San Juan de la Cruz in 1588, in a picturesque countryside on the banks of the river Eresma. The Carmelite Saint's tomb is kept there.

Visiting hours:
From 8 a. m. to 1.30 p. m. and from 4 p. m. to 8.30 p. m.

SAN ANTONIO EL REAL. Henry IV's holiday palace, later Franciscan monastery and now a convent of Clarissa nuns. Magnificent caissoned ceilings, beautiful altarpieces and valuable Flemish triptychs.
Visiting hours:
From 10 a. m. to 2 p. m. and from 3 p. m. to sunset.
Entrance fee: 10 ptas.

SAN JUSTO. Lovely 12th century Romanic church in which magnificent mural paintings of the same period have recently been discovered. There are also other elements of artistic value. (Outside hours of worship the key may be obtained at no. 2 of the Plaza de San Justo).

SAN MARTIN. Romanic church which has some valuable pieces of sculpture and some good paintings. Situated close to the square of the same name. The capitals of the porch are exceptional.

SAN JUAN DE LOS CABALLEROS. Romanic church, today an interesting Ceramics Museum, founded by the clever artist Zuloaga.

THE CITY WALLS. They are probably as old as the city, although, quite logically, they have been repaired on several occasions. The tipycal gateways are: «Santiago or El Refugio», «San Cebrián», «San Andrés», and «Postigo del Consuelo».

LAS CANONJIAS. Streets crammed with history, with typical corners and nooks, which watched royal processions pass by and the pageantry of religious ceremonies during the time of the old cathedral of Santa Maria as from 1147; today it is a splendid urban district.

SANTA CRUZ LA REAL. This was Santo Domingo de Guzman's first foundation in Spain in 1217. The present church is a magnificent example of Gothic architecture, built by the Catholic Kings. «Santo Domingo's Cave» is preserved inside.

PALACE OF THE MARQUIS OF LOZOYA. Built in the 13th century, it has a beautiful romanic entrance although the palace was restored in the 15 th century.

PALACE OF THE MARQUIS OF ARCO. Spanish renaissance of the second half of the 16th century. It has a lovely courtyard and vestibule.

EPISCOPAL PALACE. Construction was begun during the second half of the 16 th century and was finished in the 18th century by the Bishop of Segovia, Doctor Murillo.

CASA DE LOS PICOS. An original Segovian building. Until the end of the last century the San Martín gate in the city wall was attached to the façade of the house.

TURRET OF THE ARIAS-DAVILA PALACE.
Built in the 15 th century in front of what was
then the palace of King Henry IV. The finish
and the slim outlines of the tower are
exceptional.

TURRET OF THE LOZOYA PALACE. It is
situated in one of the most beautiful urban
set ups in the city, the Plaza de San Martín.

CASA DE JUAN CASCALES. Built in the
15 th century, it has some lovely slate «aji-
mez» and ancient graphite worked façade. It
forms part of a lovely corner in the centre
of the city.

HOTELES-HOTELS-HOTELS

Segovia

ACUEDUCTO. P. Claret, 4. Telf. 4890. H***
GRAN HOTEL LAS SIRENAS. Juan Bravo, 30.
Telf. 1897. H***
VICTORIA. Mayor, 5. Telf. 2181. H*
ALCAZAR. Fernández, 2. Telf. 1994. H**
CASAS. Cronista Lecea, 9. Telf. 2107. H**
COMERCIO EUROPEO. Militón, 3. Teléfo-
no 2039. H**
FLORIDA. Santa, 2. Telf. 1854. H**
JUAN BRAVO. Juan Bravo, 12. Telf. 4287.
HR**
MADRID. Muerte y Vida, 15. Telf. 4675.
P*
SOL CRISTINA. Obispo Quesada, 38 H*
VIZCAINOS. San Francisco, 12. Telf. 3185.
H*

Boceguillas

CASTILL. Ctra. General, Km. 118. Telf. 7.
P*

Castillejo de Mesleón

ANCLA. Ctra. núm. 1, Madrid-Irún, Km. 110.
H*

El Espinar

VENTA LOS PICOS. Cabezuelo. Telf. 57. H**
LA TIPICA. Pl. de España, 3. Telf. 102. H*

La Lastrilla

VENTA MAGULLO. Ctra. de Soria, Km. 195.
Telf. 2085. H**

Nava de la Asunción

HERRANZ. Real, 32. Telf. 16. H*

Navas de San Antonio

EL CORZO. Ctra. de La Coruña, Km. 75. Te-
léfono 25. H*
RUMA. Ctra. Madrid-La Coruña, Km. 75.
Telf. 11. H*

Riaza

LA TRUCHA. Avda. Doctor Tapia. Teléfono 71 82 83. H**
CASAQUEMADA. Isidro Rodríguez, 18. Teléfono 35. H*
LOS ROBLES. Hospital, 6. Telf. 41. H*

San Ildefonso o La Granja

EUROPEO. España, 9 y 10. Telf. 25. H*

San Rafael (EL ESPINAR)

LUCIA. Ctra. La Coruña, Km. 62. Telf. 23. H*
AVENIDA. Ctra. La Coruña, Km. 62. Telé-
fono 21. H**
MADRID. Avda. Perteguer, s/n. Telf. 2. H**
TELEFONICA. Ctra. La Coruña, Km. 62. Te-
léfono 138. H*

Villacastín

ALBERGUE NACIONAL DE CARRETERA.
Ctra. Nal. IV. Madrid-La Coruña. Telf. 41.
H***
HOSTERIA DEL PILAR. Ctra. La Coruña.
Telf. 39. H*
MIRASIERRA. Ctra. La Coruña, 82. Telf. 18.
H*
SAN SEBASTIAN. Ctra. Madrid-La Coruña,
Km. 84. H**
BUENOS AIRES. Ctra. La Coruña, Km. 84.
Telf. 77. H*
CASA AYUSO. Ctra. La Coruña, Km. 84.
Telf. 94. P*
LOS FAROLES. Ctra. La Coruña, Km. 83.
Telf. 74. P*
PEÑON. Ctra. La Coruña, Km. 82. Telf. 44.
H*
TEJADILLA. Ctra. La Coruña, Km. 84. Te-
léfono 66. P*

APARTAMENTOS
TURISTICOS
CAMPING
CAMPING SITES

CAMPING «FLORIDA». Primera categoría.
Carretera Segovia-La Granja, Km. 3. Tem-
porada: Junio-Septiembre.
CAMPING «MADRID-NOROESTE» Primera

categoría. Carretera Madrid-La Coruña, en San Rafael, a 30 Km. de Segovia. Temporada: Junio-Septiembre.

RESTAURANTES-RESTAURANTS RESTAURANTS

Segovia

MESON DE CANDIDO. Pl. Azoguejo, 5.
DUQUE. Cervantes, 12.
EL SEÑORIO DE CASTILLA. Pl. de Franco, 11.
AMADO. Avda. Fernández Ladreda, 9
EL BERNARDINO. Cervantes, 2.
LA CRIOLLA. Ruiz de Alda, 4.
GALICIA. Santa Columba, 3.
GARRIDO. Ruiz de Alda, 2.
LAGO. Plaza de Franco, 4.
MESON-CITO. Fernán García, 17.
LA OFICINA. Cronista Lecea, 10.
EL PINGÜINO. Ochoa Ondategui, 3.
EL RACIMO DE ORO. San Juan, 14.
RICARDO. Azoguejo, 3.
SOLAIRE. Santa Engracia, 3.
LA TAURINA. Franco, 9.
EL ABUELO. Alhóndiga, 1.
CASA BASILIO. Herrería, 8
CASA MUÑOZ. Ochoa Ondategui, 17.
CORREOS. Pl. San Facundo, 4.
HOGAR SINDICAL. Coches, 1.
BAR LAZARO. Infanta Isabel, 3.
ORENSANO. Infanta Isabel, 6
LAS PALMERAS. Pl. La Rubia, 1.
EL PORVENIR. Ochoa Ondategui, 11.
POSTIGO. Ochoa Ondategui, 7.

Ayllón

PEMAR. Pl. Mayor, 9.

Boceguillas

EL PINAR.

Cantalejo

CASA MARINO. Pl. de Franco, 4.

Cuéllar

CURRO. Pl. Mayor, 7.
FLORIDA. Paseo San Francisco, s/n.

El Espinar

LA TERRAZA. Iglesia, 24.
AVENIDA. General Mola, 6.
EL ROLAR. Pl. Cristo Rey, 7.

Honrubia de la Cuesta

MESON LAS CAMPANAS DEL MILIARIO. Ctra. Madrid-Irún, Km. 135.

La Lastrilla

LA VENTA MINA. Ctra. de Sepúlveda, s/n.

Martín Muñoz de las Posadas

LOS ROSALES. Ctra. Adanero-Gijón, Kilómetro, 116.

Navas de San Antonio

SAN ANTONIO. Príncipe, 12.

Prádena

LAS TRES BBB. Plaza, 22.

Riaza

LA TAURINA. Provencio, 5.

San Ildefonso

MADRID. Plaza de la Fruta, 1.
MARIBEN. Cuartel Nuevo, 12.
ROMA. Puerta de Segovia.
SEGOVIA. Infantes, 1.
LA TERRAZA. Puerta de Segovia, 2.
LOS CLAVELES. José Costa, 3.
MIAMI. José Costa, 1.

San Rafael

LOS ANGELES. Ctra. Madrid-Segovia, Kilómetro 70.
CASA HILARIO. Alto de los Leones, Km. 56.
POLO. Ctra. de La Coruña, s/n.
TERPA. Avda. Capitán Perteguer, s/n.

Santo Tomé del Puerto

VENTA DE JUANILLA. Sto. Tomé del Puerto, s/n.

Sepúlveda

CASA POSTIGO. José Antonio, 1.

Valsaín

CASA HILARIA. Ctra. Madrid, Km. 73.

ESPECIALIDADES GASTRONOMICAS

Gozan de justa fama los asados de cochinillos o de corderos lechales, en los cuales los hornos de la ciudad y provincia llegan a una perfección inigualable. Las truchas de Valsaín, ya elogiadas en tiempos de Carlos V; los cangrejos y las ancas de rana constituyen lo más destacable de la aportación de los ríos al buen yantar segoviano. Estos platos típicos se completan con la no menos famosa sopa castellana del siglo XV; con los judiones de La Granja, la ternera de Prádena o el chorizo de Cantimpalos.

La dulcería es excelente. El ponche segoviano y las yemas son sus máximos exponentes.

SPECIALITES GASTRONOMIQUES

Les rôtis de cochons de lait ou d'agneaux de lait jouissent d'une juste renommée, et les fours de la ville et de la province y parviennent à une perfection inégalable. Les truites de Valsaín, dont les éloges remontent déjà aux temps de Carlos Quint; les écrivisses et les cuisses de grenouilles constituent la partie la plus importante de l'apport des rivières à la bonne table de Ségovie. Ces mets typiques sont complétés par la non moins fameuse soupe Castillane du XVᵉ s.; avec les «Judiones» de La Granja, le veau de Prádena ou le chorizo de Cantimpalos.

La confiserie est excellente. Le punch de Ségovie et les «Yemas» constituent les plus importantes exposants dans ce domaine.

GASTRONOMICAL SPECIALITIES

The roasts of Suckling pig or lamb enjoy a deserved prestige as the oven roasting technique both in the city and the province has reached an unsurpassed level of perfection. Valsaín trouts, already praised in times of Carlos V; regional rivers have most sharply contributed to Segovia's good food with frog legs and crabs. These typical dishes are complemented by the famous XV th Century Castillian Soup; La Granja beans casserole, Prádena veal and sausages from Cantimpalos.

The range of sweets is excellent. Segovian punch (ponche) and eggnog biscuits (yema) are its most eulogized examples.

CAFES-BARES
CAFES-BARS
CAFE-BARS

ALTAMIRA. Avda. Fernández Ladreda, 8. Telf. 4001.
CASTILLA. Juan Bravo, 72. Telf. 3016.
CORREOS. San Facundo, 3. Telf. 2023.
JUAN BRAVO. Pl. de Franco, 8. Telf. 3000.
LA SUIZA. Pl. de Franco, 11. Telf. 3001.
LA TAURINA. Pl. de Franco, 7. Telf. 3008.
LA TROPICAL. Cervantes, 19. Telf. 3041.
LAS VEGAS. Fernán García. 17. Telf. 3057.
LOS FAROLES. Avenida Fernández Ladreda, 4. Tlf. 3056.
NEGRESCO. Pl. de Franco, 13. Telf. 2822.
PEÑALARA. Cervantes, 24. Telf. 3025.
RICARDO. Azoguejo, 3. Telf. 3033.
SOLAIRE. Santa Engracia, 3. Telf. 3419.
SOL-CRISTINA. Obispo Quesada, 14. Teléfono 2090.
SOTO. Pl. Alto de los Leones, 3. Telf. 3059.
RIO. José Zorrilla, 45. Telf. 4024.

CAFETERIAS
CAFETERIAS
CAFETERIAS

BRASIL. San Francisco, 28. Telf. 3089.
LAGO. Pl. de Franco, 4. Telf. 3085.
LA MECA. Avda. Fernández Ladreda, 12. Telf. 3060.
MARBELLA. Infanta Isabel, 14. Telf. 4022.
MARFIL. Pl. de Franco, 8. Telf. 3070.
ORLY. Bajada del Carmen. 2. Telf. 4078.
ROMA. San Francisco, 1. Telf. 4004.

TERRAZAS
TERRASSES
TERRACES

JARDIN «LAS VEGAS». Fernán García, 17. Telf. 1502.
JARDIN SAN ROQUE. Paseo de Don Ezequiel González. Telf. 2547.
JARDIN SOLAIRE. Santa Engracia, 3. Teléfono 3419.
TERRAZA - JARDIN. Santa Isabel.

TABERNAS TIPICAS
TAVERNES TYPIQUES
TYPICAL TAVERNS

EL CARRO. Dr. Sancho, 7.
LA POSADA (TASCA). Judería Vieja, 3 y 5. Telf. 4026.

VENTORROS
GUINGUETES
INNS

CHAMBERI. Carretera San Ildefonso, Km. 1.
EL ARCO. Carretera Segovia-Zamora.
MAGULLO. Carretera Soria-Plasencia, Km. 2.
Telf. 2085.
PUENTE DE HIERRO. Carretera Villacastín.
Telf. 2340.
SAN PEDRO ABANTO. Carretera Segovia-
Zamora, Km. 2. Telf. 2253.
VILLA ANGELA. Carretera San Rafael núm. 3.
Telf. 1871.
VILLA ROSA. Carretera Segovia-Zamora.

LIBRERIAS
LIBRAIRIES
BOOKSHOPS

CERVANTES. Calle de Cervantes, 16. Telé-
fono 3913.
EL ALCAZAR. Marqués del Arco, 12. Telé-
fono 3475.
ESCOLAR. San Frutos, 5.
HERRANZ. Pl. de Franco, 5. Telf. 3333.
HERRANZ. San Francisco, 6. Telf. 2662.
LA FUENCISLA. Juan Bravo, 56. Telf. 2527.
MARTIN. Juan Bravo, 20. Telf. 2232.
RASA. Juan Bravo, 31.
VDA. MAURO LOZANO. Juan Bravo, 32.
Telf. 2071.
VICENTE SOTERAS. Pl. de Franco, 11.
PAPELERIA ISA. Cervantes, 7.
JOSE ANTONIO. Avda. José Antonio, 34.
MARIA. Juan Bravo, 19.
MARIANO ALBA. Pl. de Franco, 11.

CORREOS, TELEGRAFOS
Y TELEFONOS
POSTES, TELEGRAPHES ET
TELEPHONES
POST OFFICE, TELEGRAMS
AND TELEPHONES

CORREOS. Pl. Dr. Laguna, 5. Telf. 1598.
Lista de 9 a 14 y de 17 a 19.
TELEGRAFOS. Pl. del Dr. Laguna, 5. Telf. 2137.
TELEFONOS. Pl. de los Huertos. Telf. 03.

CENTROS OFICIALES
CENTRES OFFICIELS
OFFICIAL DEPARTMENTS

AYUNTAMIENTO. Pl. de Franco, 1. Telé-
fono. 1892.
DIPUTACION PROVINCIAL. San Agustín, 23.
Telf. 2397.
GOBIERNO CIVIL. Pl. del Seminario, 1.
Telf. 1470.

GOBIERNO MILITAR. Coronel Rexach. Telé-
fono 1473.
DELEGACION PROVINCIAL DE INFORMA-
CION Y TURISMO. Pl. San Facundo, 2.
Telf. 1792.
OFICINA DE INFORMACION Y TURISMO.
Pl. de Franco, 8. Telf. 1602.
JUZGADO DE GUARDIA. San Agustín, 20.
Telf. 1801.

TELEFONOS DE URGENCIA
TELEPHONES D'URGENCE
EMERGENCY TELEPHONES

PARQUE DE INCENDIOS. Telf. 2124.
CASA DE SOCORRO. Telf. 2427.
CLINICA «18 DE JULIO». Telf. 3495.
GUARDIA CIVIL. Telf. 4590.
POLICIA. Telf. 2084.

AGENCIAS DE VIAJES
AGENCES DE VOYAGE
TRAVEL AGENCIES

SIERRAMAR. Avda. Fernández Ladreda, 11.
Telf. 1447.
ACUEDUCTO. Azoguejo, 3. Telf. 4688.

COMUNICACIONES
COMMUNICATIONS
COMMUNICATIONS

Ferrocarriles-Chemins de Fer-Railroads

DESPACHO CENTRAL DE RENFE. Pl. de
Franco, 8. Telf. 1541.

Autobuses-Autobus-Buses

LA SEPULVEDANA. Ezequiel González, 21.
Telf. 2526.
LA SERRANA, S. L. Escultor Marinas, 5.
Telf. 2033.
GALO ALVAREZ. Ezequiel González, 31.
Telf. 4614.
GARRIDO. Carretera de Sepúlveda.
LA RAPIDA. Carretera de Sepúlveda. Telé-
fono 3301.

TAXIS

Pl. de Franco. Telf. 3063.
Pl. del Azoguejo. Telf. 3062.
Avda. Fernández Ladreda (Gran turismo).
Telf. 3044.

ALQUILER DE AUTOMOVILES
LOCATION D'AUTOMOBILES
AUTOMOBILE RENTALS

SIERRAMAR. Fernández Ladreda, 11. Teléfono 1447.
GALVAN. Puente de Muerte y Vida, 6. Telf. 1820.

TALLERES DE REPARACION
DE AUTOMOVILES
ATELIERS DE REPARATION
D'AUTOMOBILES
AUTO REPAIR GARAGES

BARREIROS, SIMCA, DODGE, MOTOR NACIONAL, S. A. (MOSA). Carretera San Rafael (Cerro de la Horca). Telf. 4693.
CITROEN. GARAJE ESPAÑA. Victoria, 1. Telf. 1405 y 2120.
RENAULT. EMAIZA. Carretera Cuéllar, s/n.
SEAT, FIAT. Garaje Sousa. Paseo Ezequiel González, 12. Telf. 1858.
PABLO DE SOUSA. Paseo Ezequiel González, 12. Telf. 1953. (Volswagen, peugeot).
NUEVO TALLER. Paseo Ezequiel González, 12. Telf. 3286.
GARAJE GOMEZ. Carretera de Arévalo. Teléfono 2647. (DKW-Mercedes).
RENAULT. Carretera Boceguillas, 2. Telf. 1906.
SAN FRUTOS. San Vicente Ferrer, 8. Teléfono 3410. (Sava-Austin).
AURELIO HERNANDEZ. Alto de Santo Tomás, 2. Telf. 3275 (Borgward).

ESTACIONES DE SERVICIO
POSTE D'ESENCE
SERVICE STATIONS

SEGOVIA. Carretera Estación F. C. Segovia a Fuencisla.
SEGOVIA. Carretera Madrid-Segovia, Km. 93,6
SEGOVIA. Carretera Villalba-Segovia, Km. 49,8.
SEGOVIA. Carretera San Rafael, confluencia Avda. José Antonio.
AGUILAFUENTE. Pl. de la Fuente.
BOCEGUILLAS. Carretera Madrid-Irún, Km. 117,3.
CANTALEJO. Carretera Segovia-Aranda de Duero, Km. 4,7.
CARBONERO EL MAYOR. Carretera Madrid-Valladolid, Km. 104.
CEREZO DE ABAJO. Carretera Madrid-Irún, Km. 102,7.
CUELLAR. Carretera Madrid-León, por Segovia, Km. 147,7.
NAVAS DE LA ASUNCION. Carretera Cuéllar a Arévalo, Km. 32,7.
SAN RAFAEL. Carretera Madrid-La Coruña, Km. 62,4.

TUREGANO. Carretera Aranda-Segovia, Km. 33,7.
VILLACASTIN. Carretera Madrid-La Coruña, Km. 83,3.

TEATROS Y CINES
THEATRES ET CINEMAS
THEATRES AND CINEMAS

TEATRO CERVANTES. Cervantes, 1. Teléfono 2101.
TEATRO JUAN BRAVO. Pl. de Franco, 7. Telf. 2860.
CINE «LAS SIRENAS». Juan Bravo, 30. Telf. 1503.
CINE VICTORIA. Gobernador F. Jiménez, 6. Telf. 2936.

SALAS DE FIESTAS
CABARETS
NIGHT CLUBS

SKOWKING. Avda. Fernández Ladreda, 2.
LAS VEGAS. Fernán García, 17.
FLORIDA. Paseo del Salón, s/n.
LAS SIRENAS. Juan Bravo, 30.
CUEVAS DEL DUQUE. Santa Engracia, 2.
CUAVAS DE ALTAMIRA. Avda. Fernández Ladreda, 2.
TERRAZA JARDIN. (Solo verano), Larpa, s/n.

CLUBS Y SOCIEDADES
DEPORTIVAS
CLUBS ET SOCIETES
SPORTIVES
CLUBS AND SPORT
SOCIETIES

CASINO DE LA UNION. Juan Bravo, 6. Telf. 2252.
CLUB RECREATIVO CULTURAL. Bajada del Carmen, 2. Telf. 3295.
CIRCULO «SAGRADA FAMILIA». Avda. de José Antonio, 32. Telf. 3235.
SOCIEDAD GIMNASTICA SEGOVIANA. San Agustín, 2.
SOCIEDAD DE CAZADORES Y PESCADORES. Avda. Fernández Ladreda, 4. Telf. 1964.
SOCIEDAD CICLISTA SEGOVIANA. Avda. Padre Claret, 10. Telf. 4203.
SOCIEDAD DEPORTIVA EXCURSIONISTA. Muerte y Vida, 15.

BANCOS-BANQUES-BANKS

BANCO DE ESPAÑA. Ildefonso Rodríguez, 1. Telf. 3996.
BANCO CASTELLANO. Azoguejo, 9. Teléfono 2041.

BANCO ESPAÑOL DE CREDITO. Cervantes, 27. Telf. 4295.

BANCO HISPANO AMERICANO. Avda. Fernández Ladreda, 4. Telf. 4595.

BANCO CENTRAL. Avda. Fernández Ladreda, 15. Telf. 4190.

CAJA DE AHORROS. Avda. Fernández Ladreda, 2. Telf. 4490.

BANCO SALAMANCA. Avda. Fernández Ladreda, 9.

ARCHIVOS Y BIBLIOTECAS
ARCHIVES ET BIBLIOTHEQUES
ARCHIVES AND LIBRARIES

ARCHIVO HISTORICO. Calle de Juan Bravo, 13. Telf. 1859.

ARCHIVO MUNICIPAL. Edificio de la Alhóndiga.

ARCHIVO GENERAL MILITAR. Edificio del Alcázar. Telf. 1516.

ARCHIVO CATEDRALICIO. Catedral. Teléfono 4307.

PALACIO DE ARCHIVOS Y BIBLIOTECAS. Juan Bravo, 13.

ANTICUARIOS-ANTIQUAIRES
ANTIQUE SHOPS

ANTIGÜEDADES LA FUENCISLA. Isabel la Católica, 12. Telf. 1824.

ANTIGÜEDADES ESCRIBANO. Pl. Conde Cheste (Junto a la escuela Normal de Magisterio).

ANTIGÜEDADES SIMON «VILORIA LLORENTE». Pl. de los Huertos.

MUSEOS-MUSÉES-MUSEUMS

MUSEO CATEDRALICIO. Pl. de Franco.
Horas de visita:
Verano: de 9 a 18 horas.
Invierno: de 9 a 13 y de 15 a 18 horas.
Precio entrada: 10 pesetas.

MUSEO ZULOAGA (Cerámica). Pl. Colmenares, 4.
Horas de visita:
Verano: de 10,30 a 13, 30 y de 16, 30 a 19.
Invierno: de 10,30 a 13,30 y de 16,30 a 18.
Precio de entrada: 15 Ptas. Cerrado los lunes.

MUSEO PROVINCIAL. San Agustín, 8.
Horas de visita:
Verano: de 10,30 a 13,30 y de 15,30 a 19.
Invierno: de 10,30 a 13,30 y de 16,30 a 18.
Precio de entrada: 5 Ptas. Cerrado los lunes.

CAZA Y PESCA

CAZA. Abunda en la provincia de Segovia la perdiz roja e igualmente la liebre y el conejo, en el período que comprende desde primeros de octubre al primer domingo de febrero.

Para las especies codorniz, tórtola y paloma, la temporada de caza es desde la primera quincena de agosto hasta el 10 de septiembre. Los pinares de la provincia suelen ser en la época de paso de torcaces, lugares de buenas cacerías, como también las lagunas diseminadas por la tierra segoviana suelen albergar, en época de emigración, patos salvajes y otras aves palmípedas.

No existen actualmente más que cotos y vedados particulares.

PESCA. La especie común de trucha se pesca en el río Moros, río Cega, arroyo de Valsaín, río Cambrones, río Pirón, arroyo del Fraile, arroyo Galindo, arroyo Viejo, etc. Además de la trucha común existen buenos ejemplares de la trucha «Arco Iris». Asimismo se ha comprobado la existencia de un tipo de trucha distinta que se denomina «Plateada».

Existen cuatro cotos de pesca deportiva:

COTO DE PUENTE ALTA (Término de Revenga). Lo constituye el embalse del agua potable de Segovia, expendiendo los permisos el Guarda del Servicio de Pesca en el mismo pantano; su importe es de 50 pesetas. Máximo de piezas pescadas, 15; el peso normal de las piezas es de 300 gramos, llegando en ocasiones a los dos y tres kilogramos. Se pueden utilizar cebos naturales y artificiales.

COTO DEL RIO ERESMA (Término de Palazuelos). La expedición de permisos se realiza en el Servicio de Pesca de Segovia, al precio de 100 pesetas, con un tope de 15 truchas por permiso. La pesca se realiza los martes, jueves, domingos y festivos. Se cobran piezas de buen tamaño.

COTO ARROYO VIEJO (Término de Collado-Hermoso). Los permisos, con limitación a seis diarios, cuestan 50 pesetas. Pesca los martes, jueves, sábados, domingos y festivos. Las truchas son de menor tamaño.

COTO DE CEGA (Término de Navafría). El precio del permiso es el de 50 pesetas, siendo el límite de las piezas a pescar, 20. Se expiden diariamente cuatro permisos por el Servicio de Pesca de Segovia, autorizándose únicamente cebos artificiales. Las truchas son abundantes, pero pequeñas.

Los barbos existen en abundancia en el pantano de Burgomillodo, río Moros, río Duratón, río Riaza y pantano de Linares, próximo a Maderuelo, y en el río Eresma. Puede asegurarse que la mayor parte de los ríos y arroyos de Segovia, reúnen inmejorables condiciones para la pesca del cangrejo, por lo que la provincia de Segovia está clasificada entre las cuatro o cinco provincias cangrejeras de España. Se pescan en los ríos: Moros, Pirón, Cega, Eresma y Duratón y en los arroyos Matilla, Santa Ana, etcétera.

La temporada es desde el 15 de junio al 15 de septiembre.

CHASSE ET PÊCHE

CHASSE. Abonde dans la province de Ségovie, en ce qui concerne la perdrix rouge, le lièvre et le lapin, dans la période qui va du début d'octobre au premier dimanche de février. Pour les cailles, tourterelles et pigeons, la saison de chasse va et la première quinzaine d'août au 10 septembre. Les pinèdes de la province sont, lors du passage des ramiers, des lieux de bonne chasse, ainsi que les lagunes disséminées sur la terre ségovienne, qui abritent à l'époque de l'émigration des canards sauvages et d'autres palmipèdes. Actuellement, il n'existe que des chasses particulières.

PÊCHE. L'espèce commune de truite se pêche dans le ruisseau Moros, le Cega, le Valsain, le Cambrones, le Pirón, le ruisseau del Fraile, le Galindo, le Viejo, etc. Outre la truite commune, il existe de bons exemplaires de la truite «Arc en ciel». On a également constaté l'existence d'un type de truite distinct qui s'appelle «argentée». Il y a quatre réserves de pêche sportive:

COTO DE PUENTE ALTA (Territoire de Revenga). Constitué par le barrage d'eau potable de Ségovie, les permis étants octroyés par le Garde du Service de Pêche, au barrage même. Son montant est de 50 ptas. Maximum de pièces pêchées: 15. Le poids normal des pièces est de 300 gr. et atteint parfois deux et trois kg. On peut utiliser des appâts naturels et artificiels.

COTO DEL RIO ERESMA (Territoire de Palazuelos). Les permis sont obtenus au Service de Pêche de Ségovie, au prix de 100 ptas. avec un maximum de 15 truites par permis; la pêche se fait les mardis, jeudis, dimanches et jours de fête. On pêche des pièces de bonne taille.

COTO ARROYO VIEJO (Territoire de Collado-Hermoso). Les permis, avec limitation de six par jour, coûtent 50 ptas. Pêche les mardis jeudis, samedis et dimanches, et jours de fête. Les truites sont plus petites.

COTO DEL CEGA (Territoire de Navafría). Le prix du permis est de 50 ptas., et la limite de 20 pièces. On donne journellement 4 permis, par le Service de Pêche de

Ségovie, autorisant uniquement les appâts artificiels. Les truites sont abondantes mais petites.

Les barbeaux existent en abondance dans le barrage de Burgomillodo le ruisseau Moros, le Duratón, le Riaza et le barrage de Linares, près de Maderuelo, et le ruisseau Eresma.

On peut affirmer que le plupart des ruisseaux et rivières le Ségovie réunissent les meilleures conditions pour la pêche de l'écrevisse, ce qui classe la province de Ségovie parmi les 4 ou 5 plus productrices d'écrevisses en Espagne. On pêche dans les cours d'eau: Moros, Pirón, Cega, Eresma, et Duratón, ainsi que le Matilla, Santa Ana, etc. La saison dure du 15 juin au 15 septembre.

HUNTING AND FISHING

HUNTING, SHOOTING. There is a great deal of partridge, hare and rabbit in the province of Segovia, during the season from the beginning of October to the first Sunday in February.

For quail, turtle-doves and pigeons, the shooting season is from the first fortnight in August to the 10th September. During the season when the queest are passing through, the pine forets in the province are excellent shooting grounds. Also the lakes, spread out over the province, usually provide wild duck and other webfooted birds during the emmigration season.

At the moment there are only private reserves.

FISHING. The common of species of trout is fished in the river Moros, river Cega, and Valsaín stream. Also river Cambrones, river Pirón, Fraile stream, Galinda stream, Viejo stream, etc. Apart from ordinary trout there are some species of «Rainbow» trout. The existence of another species of trout has also been discovered, i. e. the «silver» trout.

There are four fishing reserves:

COTO DE PUENTE ALTA (In the Revenga municipality). This consists of the drinking water reservoir for Segovia and permits are issued by the Fishing Guard Service at the reservoir. The permit costs 50 ptas. Maximum no, of fish 15; the normal weight of the fish is 300 grs. sometimes reaching two or there kilos. Natural or artificial bait may be used.

COTO DEL RIO ERESMA (In the municipality of Palazuelos). Permits are issued by the Segovia Fishing Service, at the price of Ptas. 100, with a maximum of 15 trout per permit. Fishing is held on Tuesdays, Thursdays, Sundays, and holidays. Good sized fich can be caught.

COTO ARROYO VIEJO (in Collado-Hermoso). Fishing permits are limited to 6 a day and cost 50 pesetas. Fishing is allowed Tuesdays, Thursdays, Saturdays and holidays. The trout are small.

COTO DEL CEGA (in Navafria). Fishing permits cost 50 pesetas and the limit of fish is set at 20. 4 permits a day are sold by the Fishing Service of Segovia. Only artificial bait is allowed. Trout are abundant but small.

Barbels are found in abundance in the Burgomillodo Dam, the Moros River, the Duratón River, the Riaza River and the Linares Dam near Maderuelo and the Eresma River.

You can be assured that the majority of rivers and creeks in Segovia are excellent for crab fishing. The province of Segovia is classified along with 4 or 5 others as the best in Spain for crabs. They are cought in the rivers: Pirón, Cega, Eresma, and Duratón and in Matilla Creek and Santa Ana Creek, etc. The crab season is from June 15 to September 15.

FIESTAS POPULARES Y REGIONALES

AGUILAFUENTE. Ferias y fiestas, del 15 al 17 de agosto. Atracciones, bailes, toros, etc. A 35 Km. de Segovia.

AYLLON. Fiestas tradicionales los dias 29 y 30 de septiembre. Corridas de toros y otros festejos. Del 7 al 11 de noviembre, feria de marcado tipismo. A 94 Km. de Segovia.

CANTIMPALOS. Fiestas de la Inmaculada Concepción el 24 de septiembre. Bailes, becerros, etc. A 20 Km. de Segovia.

CARBONERO EL MAYOR. Feria de San José, 19 al 22, de marzo. El dia 4 de septiembre, fiesta de la virgen del Bustar; romería tipica, novilladas, etc., a 25 Km. de Segovia.

COCA. Fiestas de la Cruz de Mayo, el dia 3. Festejos deportivos, toros, bailes públicos, conciertos, etc. Del 15 al 18 de agosto, fiestas de Nuestra Señora del Rosario y San Roque. A 47 Km. de Segovia.

CUELLAR. Fiesta patronales, del 20 al 30 de agosto. Típicos encierros que se celebran desde el siglo XV, corridas de toros, tradicionales «limonadas» y «pandas». El 17 de septiembre, famosa romería en el Santuario de la Virgen del Henar, a 5 Km. de Cuéllar. Procesión de antorchas y festejos populares. A 60 Km. de Segovia.

EL ESPINAR. Fiestas del Cristo del Caloco, el 8 de septiembre. Procesión, romerías, bailes de trajes regionales, conciertos y toros. Del 22 al 28 de octubre, fiestas patronales de San Rafael. El 24 se celebran en el barrio de San Rafael, con bailes públicos y fiestas taurinas. A 35 Km. de Segovia.

FUENTEPELAYO. Fiestas de San Miguel el dia 8 de mayo con romería a la ermita titular. Durante la octava del Corpus, grandes fiestas con paloteo típico, danzas, etc., de gran sabor y carácter. Los dias 29 y 30 de septiembre, fiestas de San Miguel. Novilladas, encierros, etc. A 39 Km. de Segovia.

NAVA DE LA ASUNCION. Fiestas del Santísimo Cristo de la Expiación el 20 de septiembre. Novillada y otros festejos populares. A 40 Km. de Segovia.

PEDRAZA DE LA SIERRA. Fiestas de Nuestra Señora del Carrascal del 8 al 10 de septiembre. Toros, bailes, etc. Ambiente muy típico. A 33 Km. de Segovia.

RIAZA. Ferias del Angel, del 1 al 5 de marzo. Folklore de la Sierra. El 10 de septiembre, famosa romería a la ermita de la Virgen de Hontanares. Toros, bailes, fiestas religiosas y profanas. Del 25 al 30 de octubre, feria de ganados. A 74 Km. de Segovia.

SAN ILDEFONSO. Fiestas de San Luis, dia 25 de agosto. Gigantes y cabezudos, verbenas, tiro de pichón y al plato. Juegos de agua en las monumentales fuentes de los jardines.

SANTA MARIA LA REAL DE NIEVA. Fiestas de la Virgen de la Soterraña del 7 al 12 de septiembre. Procesión, ofrenda de cirios, de gran emotividad, partidos de pelota, bailes, toros, etc. A 30 Km. de Segovia.

SEGOVIA. Semana Santa: solemnes procesiones, especialmente interesante la del Viernes Santo por la belleza y valor de las imágenes. Ferias y Fiestas de San Juan y San Pedro del 24 al 29 de junio. Gigantes y cabezudos, dianas, verbenas, toros, ferial de ganados, deportes, carreras de motos y bicicletas, concursos, natación, etc. Durante el año se celebran otras fiestas tradicionales como las romerías de San Marcos y la Cruz, los dias 25 de abril y 3 de mayo; fiestas de San Roque en el barrio de San Millán; fiestas de la Catorcena, y el primer domingo de septiembre y las fiestas de las parroquias con diversos festejos religiosos y populares.

SEPULVEDA. Fiestas patronales los dias 25 y 26 de agosto. Toros, encierros, bailes, etc. A 60 Km. de Segovia.

TUREGANO. Ferias del 1 al 4 de diciembre. Gran feria de ganados, animado tipismo. A 34 Km. de Segovia.

VILLACASTIN. Romería de la Virgen del Carrascal, Patrona de la villa, el 4 de mayo, con diversos actos típicos. Del 18 al 20 de septiembre, feria de ganado, con bailes típicos. Del 27 al 29 Fiestas de San Sebastián Mártir; novillada, carreras, bailes de gaita y tamboril.

ZAMARRAMALA. Fiestas de Santa Agueda, declaradas de interés turístico. Alcaldesas, procesión, baile de rueda. Muy famosas. El día 5 de febrero o el domingo más inmediato a dicha fecha. Muy próxima a Segovia.

ZARZUELA DEL MONTE. Fiestas de San Vicente Mártir del 22 al 25 de enero. Danzas y bailes típicos. A 27 Km. de Segovia.

FÊTES POPULAIRES ET REGIONALES

AGUILAFUENTE. Fêtes et foires, du 15 au 17 août, attractions, danses, taureaux, etc. A 35 Km. de Ségovie.

AYLLON. Fêtes traditionnelles les 29 et 30 septembre. Corridas de taureaux et autres manifestations. Du 7 au 11 novembre, fête très typique. A 94 Km. de Ségovie.

CANTIMPALOS. Fête de l'Immaculée Conception le 24 septembre. Danses, petits taureaux, etc. A 20 Km. de Ségovie.

CARBONERO EL MAYOR. Fête de St. Joseph, 19 au 22 mars. Le 4 septembre fête de la Vierge du Bustar; procession typique, courses de novillos, etc. A 25 Km. de Ségovie.

COCA. Fêtes de la Croix de Mai, le 3. Manifestations sportives, taureaux, bals publics, concerts, etc. Du 15 au 18 août, fêtes, de N. D. du Rosaire et Saint Roch. A 47 Km. de Ségovie.

CUELLAR. Fêtes patronales, du 20 au 30 août. Lâcher de taureaux dans les rues, depuis le XVᵉ s., corridas, traditionnels «limonadas» et «Pandas». Le 17 septembre, fameuse procession au sanctuaire de la Vierge du Henar, à 5 Km. de Cuéllar. Procession aux flambeaux et fêtes populaires. A 60 Km. de Ségovie.

EL ESPINAR. Fête du Christ du Caloco, le 8 septembre. Procession, pèlerinages danses en costumes régionaux, concerts et taureaux. Du 22 au 28 octobre, fêtes patronales de St. Raphael. Le 24 elles sont célébrées dans le quartier de St. Raphael par des bals publics et des fêtes taurines. A 35 Km. de Ségovie.

FUENTEPELAYO. Fêtes de St. Michel le 8 mai avec pèlerinage à l'ermitage titulaire. Pendant la huitaine du Corpus, grandes fêtes typiques, danses, etc. de grande saveur. Les 29 et 30 septembre, fêtes de St. Michel. Courses de novillos, lâcher de taureaux, etc. A 39 Km. de Ségovie.

NAVA DE LA ASUNCION. Fêtes du Très St. Christ de l'Expiation le 20 septembre. Novillada et autres fêtes populaires. A 40 Km. de Ségovie.

PEDRAZA DE LA SIERRA. Fêtes de Notre Dame del Carrascal, du 8 au 10 septembre.

Taureaux, danses, etc. Ambiance très typique. A 33 Km. de Ségovie.

RIAZA. Fêtes de l'Ange, du 1 au 5 mars. Folklore de la Sierra. Le 10 septembre, fameuse procession à l'ermitage de la Vierge de Hontanares. Taureaux, danses, fêtes religieuses et profanes. Du 25 au 30 octobre. Foire de bétail. A 74 Km. de Ségovie.

SAN ILDEFONSO. Fête de St. Louis, 25 août. Géants et nains à grosse tête, kermesses, tir au pigeon et au plateau. Jeux d'eau dans les fontaines monumentales des jardins.

SANTA MARIA LA REAL DE NIEVA. Fêtes de la Vierge de la Soterraña du 7 au 12 septembre. Procession, offrande de cierges, très émouvante, parties de balle, danses, taureaux, etc. A 30 Km. de Ségovie.

SEGOVIE. Semaine Sainte: processions solennelles, spécialement intéressante celle du Vendredi Saint, pour la beauté et la valeur des statues. Foires et fêtes de St. Jean et St. Pierre du 24 au 29 juin. Géants et grosses têtes, dianes, kermesses, taureaux, foire de bétail, sports, courses de motos et bicyclettes, concours, natation, etc. Pendant l'année, on célèbre d'autres fêtes traditionnelles comme les pèlerinages de St. Marc et la Croix, les 25 avril et 3 mai; fêtes de St. Roch dans le quartier de St. Millan: fêtes de la Quatorzaine le premier dimanche de septembre et les fêtes des paroisses avec diverses célébrations religieuses et populaires.

SEPULVEDA. Fêtes patronales, les 25 et 26 août. Taureaux, lâcher de taureaux dans les rues, danses, etc. A 60 Km. de Ségovie.

TUREGANO. Foires du 1 au 4 décembre. Grande foire au bétail, très typique. A 34 Km. de Ségovie.

VILLACASTIN. Pèlerinage de la Vierge del Carrascal, Patronne de la ville, le 4 mai avec divers actes typiques. Du 18 au 20 septembre. Foire au bétail avec danses typiques. Du 27 au 29, fêtes de St. Sébastien martyr; novillada, courses, danses de gaita et tambourin.

ZAMARRAMALA. Fêtes de Sainte Aguéda, déclarées d'intérêt touristique. Mairesses, procession, danse en ronde. Très fameuses. Le 5 février ou le dimanche le plus immédiat de cette date. Tout près de Ségovie.

ZARZUELA DEL MONTE. Fêtes de St. Vincent Martyr du 22 au 25 janvier. Danses typiques. A 27 Km. de Ségovie.

● POPULAR AND REGIONAL FESTIVALS

AGUILAFUENTE. Fairs and festivities from 15th to 17th August. Atractions, dances, bulls, etc. 35 Km. from Segovia.

AYLLON. Traditional festivities from 29th to 30th Sept. Bullfights and other festivals.

From 7th to 11th Nov, very typical fair, 94 Km. from Segovia.

CANTIMPALOS. Festival of the Immaculate Conception on 24th September. Dances, young bullfighting, etc. 20 Km. from Segovia.

CARBONERO EL MAYOR. Festival of St. Joseph from 19th to 22nd March. On 4th September, festival of the Virgin of Bustar; typical romery, bullfights, etc., 25 Km. from Segovia.

COCA. Festivals of the Cruz de Mayo, on 3rd May. Sports, Bulls, public dances, concerts, etc. From 15th to 18th August, festival of Our Lady of the Rosary and San Roque, 47 Km. from Segovia.

CUELLAR. Festival of the patron Saint, from 20th to 30th August. Typical round ups of bulls which have been held since the 15th c., bullfights, traditional «limonadas and pandas». The 17th Sep. famous romery to the Sanctuary of the Virgin of Henar, 5 Km. from Cuéllar. Procession of torch bearers and popular festivities. 60 Km. from Segovia.

EL ESPINAR. Festivities of Christ of Caloco, on 8th Sep. Procession romeries, dances in traditional costume, concerts and bullfights. From 22nd to 28th October festival of San Rafael, the town's patron saint. On 24th, public dances and bullfights are held in the San Rafael district. 35 Km. from Segovia.

FUENTEPELAYO. Festivals of San Miguel on 8th May with romery to the hermitage. During Corpus, enormous festivities with typical stick fighting, dances etc. The festivities have a great deal of character and atmosphere. 29th and 30th September, the festival of St. Michael. Bullfights and round ups, etc. 39 Km. from Segovia.

NAVA DE LA ASUNCION. Festival of the Santisimo Cristo de la Expiación on 20th September. Bull fight and other popular festivities. 40 Km. from Segovia.

PEDRAZA DE LA SIERRA. Festival of Our Lady of Carrascal on 8th to 10th September. Bulls, dances, etc. Very typical atmosphere. 33 Km. from Segovia.

RIAZA. Festival of El Angel, from 1st to 5th March. Mountain folklore. On 10th September famous romery to the Hermitage of the Virgin of Hontanares. Bulls, dances, religious festivals and others. From 25th to 30th October, Cattle fair. 74 Km. from Segovia.

SAN ILDEFONSO. Festival of San Luis on 25th August. Giants and large headed monsters, fairs, pigeon shooting and clay pigeons. The magnificent monumental fountains in the gardens play.

SANTA MARIA LA REAL DE NIEVA. Festivals of the Virgin of Soterraña from 7th to 12th September. Procession, offering of wax candles, very emotional, pelota matches, dances, bulls, etc. 30 Km. from Segovia.

SEGOVIA. Holy Week: solemn processions, the most interesting one being on Good Friday on account of the beauty and value of the images. Fairs and Festivals of San Juan and San Pedro on 24th to 29th June. Giants and large headed monsters, reveilles, fairs, bulls, cattle market, sports, motorbike races and cycle races, competitions, swimming etc. Other traditional festivals are celebrated throughout the years such as the romeries of San Marcos and La Cruz, on 25th April and 3rd May: festivals of San Roque in the San Millán district; festival of the Catorcena, the first Sunday in September and the festivals of the parishes with different religious and popular ceremonies.

SEPULVEDA. Feast of the patron saint on 25th and 26th August. Bulls round ups, dances, etc. 60 Km. from Segovia.

TUREGANO. Festivals of 1st to 4th December. Large cattle fair, very gay atmosphere. 34 Km. from Segovia.

VILLACASTIN. Romery of the Virgin of Carrascal, Patron Saint of the town, on 4th May, with different typical ceremonies. From 18th to 20th September, cattle fair, with typical dances. From 27th to 29th Festival of San Sebastián, the martyr: bull fights, races bagpipe and tambourine dances.

ZAMARRAMALA. Festival of Santa Agueda, which has been declared of tourist interest. Mayors' wives, procession, wheel dance. Very famous. On 5th Februay or Sunday nearest to that date. Very close to Segovia.

ZARZUELA DEL MONTE. Festival of San Vicente, the martyr, on 22nd to 25th January. Dances and typical reels. 27 Km. from Segovia.

LUGARES DE MAYOR INTERES EN LA PROVINCIA

AYLLON. Villa que fue del señorío de D. Alvaro de Luna. Murallas medievales, Iglesia románica, castillo en ruinas; pintoresca plaza.

CARBONERO EL MAYOR. Notable Iglesia gótica, de tres naves, hermoso retablo y magníficas pinturas atribuidas a Rosales. A 26 Km. de la capital.

CASTILLO DE CASTILNOVO. Notable castillo medieval, sin duda el mejor conservado de la provincia. Propiedad particular.

COCA. Impresionante castillo medieval, construído por los Fonseca, estilo mudéjar. Hoy Escuela de Capataces Forestales. Interesante iglesia de estilo gótico, magníficos sepulcros de los Fonseca, labrados en alabastro. A 48 Km. de la capital.

CUELLAR. Castillo-palacio construido por D. Beltrán de la Cueva en 1464. La villa conserva notables iglesias mudéjares, restos de sus murallas, casonas blasonadas, etc.

EL ESPINAR. Iglesia de estilo herreriano, construida por Juan de Minjares; buen retablo plateresco; hermosas sardas de Sánchez Coello. A 35 Km. de la capital.

FUENTIDUEÑA. Pintoresca villa con restos de sus murallas románicas y notable iglesia de este estilo.

LA GRANJA DE SAN ILDEFONSO. Maravilloso Palacio y Jardines, mandados construir por Felipe V en 1720, según planos de Ardemáns. El Palacio atesora una de las mejores colecciones del mundo de tapices.
Horario de visita al Palacio:
De 10 a 3 y de 14 a 18 horas. Precio: 20 pesetas.
La entrada a los Jardines es libre, excepto jueves, domingos y festivos de mayo a octubre; en estos días, a partir de las 14 horas, el precio es de 15 pesetas; corriendo algunas de sus fuentes. La totalidad de ellas corren únicamente en los siguientes días: 30 de mayo y primer domingo de julio y 25 de julio. Precio 5 pesetas. 25 de agosto, festividad de San Luis de Francia, gratis. A 12 Km. de Segovia en la carretera de Madrid por Navacerrada.

MADERUELO. Villa situada en un pintoresco lugar de la sierra, próxima al pantano de Linares y al río Riaza, con abundante pesca. Ermita de la Veracruz, que poseía las magníficas pinturas románicas, que se pueden admirar hoy en el Museo del Prado.

MARTIN MUÑOZ DE LAS POSADAS. Iglesia gótica, con notable sepulcro del Cardenal Espinosa y un célebre cuadro de El Greco. Restos del Palacio de aquel personaje.

MIRADOR DEL TERMILLO. Situado a 2 Km. de la capital, en la carretera de Valladolid; desde él se contempla un maravilloso panorama de Segovia.

PEDRAZA. Pintoresca villa amurallada y con una sola puerta de acceso. Su Plaza Mayor es una de las más características de Castilla. Notable castillo medieval. Está prevista la construcción en ella de un Parador Nacional de Turismo. A 37 Km. de Segovia.

PINAR DE LA NAVA FRIA. Es uno de los pinares más espectaculares de España. A 30 Km. de la capital por la carretera de la Sierra a Riaza.

RIAZA. Centro de verano, por su privilegiada situación serrana. Característica plaza portificada e iglesia parroquial renacentista. A 72 Km. de Segovia.

RIOFRIO. Palacio real, mandado construir por Isabel de Farnesio, al subir al trono su hijo Fernando VI. El Palacio, de estilo neoclásico, tiene una buena pinacoteca, en la que destaca «La cuerna de venado», cua-

dro de Velázquez, recientemente identificado. Estupenda colección de tapices. Hermoso parque poblado de gamos y ciervos. En sus salas será abierto un Museo Nacional de Cinegética. A 10 kilómetros de la capital.

SANTA MARIA LA REAL DE NIEVA. Notable iglesia gótica, con un magnífico claustro de transición del románico al gótico. Su retablo es de estilo berruguetiano. A 30 Km. de Segovia.

SEPULVEDA. Situada en un pintoresco lugar, rodeada por los ríos Duratón y Castilla. Su casco urbano tiene un peculiar acento medieval, por sus casas blasonadas, puertas de la muralla, rincones, notables iglesias como San Justo, San Bartolomé, la Virgen de la Peña y las ruinas de su castillo. A 60 Km. de la capital.

SOTOSALBOS. Iglesia románica con notables torre y portada. Imagen románica de Nuestra Señora de la Sierra. A 18 Km. de Segovia.

TUREGANO. Es muy notable su conocida plaza porticada, señoreada por un magnífico castillo, reconstruido por el Obispo de Segovia D. Juan Arias Dávila en el siglo XV. Está fortaleza fue prisión del secretario de Felipe II, Antonio Pérez.

VILLACASTIN. Magnífico templo de estilo herreriano, obra de Fray Antonio de Villacastín, aparejador en las obras de El Escorial. Notables retablos y pinturas de Alonso de Herrera. Albergue Nacional de Carretera. A 33 Km. de Segovia, en la carretera general Madrid-La Coruña.

EL ESPINAR. Eglise de style herrérien, construite par Juan de Minjares bon retable plateresque; belles «sardas» de Sánchez Coello. A 35 Km. de la capitale.

FUENTIDUEÑA. Ville pittoresque avec des restes de ses murailles romanes et une église remarquable de ce style.

LA GRANJA DE SAN ILDEFONSO. Merveilleux Palais et Jardins, construits sur l'ordre de Philippe V en 1720 suivant les plans de Ardemans. La Palais referme une des meilleures collections du monde de tapisseries.
Heures de visite au Palais:
De 10 à 13 et de 14 à 18 h.
Prix: 20 ptas.
L'entrée aux Jardins est libre sauf les jeudis, dimanches et jours de fête de mai à octobre; ces jours-là, à partir de 14 h. le prix est de 15 ptas. Certaines fontaines coulent. La totalité coule seulement les jours suivants: 30 mai, premier dimanche de juillet et 25 juillet.
Prix: 5 ptas.
25 août, fête de St. Louis de France, gratis. A 12 Km. de Ségovie sur la route de Madrid par Navacerrada.

MADERUELO. Ville située dans un endroit pittoresque de la sierra, près de l'étang de Linares et du ruisseau Riaza, avec pêche abondante. Ermitage de la Veracruz, qui possédait les magnifiques peintures romanes que l'on peut admirer aujourd'hui au Musée du Prado.

MARTIN MUÑOZ DE LAS POSADAS. Eglise gothique avec un sépulcre remarquable du Cardinal Espinosa et un tableau célèbre du Greco. Restes du palais de ce personnage. (Espinosa).

MIRADOR DEL TERMILLO. Situé à 2 Km. de la capitale, sur la route de Valladolid, d'où l'on contemple un merveilleux panorama de Ségovie.

PEDRAZA. Pittoresque ville entourée de murailles avec une seule porte d'accès. Sa Grand Place est l'une des plus caractéristiques de Castille. Remarquable château médiéval. On prévoit la construction d'une Auberge Nationale de Tourisme. A 37 Km. de Ségovie.

PINAR DE NAVA FRIA. Est l'une des pinèdes les plus spectaculaires de l'Espagne. A 30 Km. de la capitale, par la route de la Sierra à Riaza.

RIAZA. Centre de villégiature, en raison de sa situation privilégiée dans la montagne. Place caractéristique avec portiques, et église paroissiale renaissance. A 72 Km. de Ségovie.

RIOFRIO. Palais royal construit sur l'ordre d'Isabelle de Farnèse, lorsque son fils Ferdinand VI monta sur le trône. Le Palais de style néo-classique, possède une bonne pinacothèque, ou l'on distingue «la corne de cerf» de Velázquez récemment identifiée. Magnifique collection de tapisseries. Beau parc peuplé de daims et de cerfs. Dans ses salles, on va ouvrir un Musée National de Cynégétique. A 10 Km. de la capitale.

SANTA MARIA LA REAL DE NIEVA. Remarquable église gothique avec un magnifique cloître de transition du roman au gothique. Son retable est du style de Berruguete. A 30 Km. de Ségovie.

SEPULVEDA. Située dans un endroit pittoresque, entourée par les rivières Duratón et Castilla. Son noyau urbain possède un accent médiéval particulier, avec ses maisons blasonnées les portes de la muraille, les recoins, et des églises remarquables comme St. Juste, St. Barthélemy, la Vierge de la Peña et les ruines de son château. A 60 Km. de la capitale.

SOTOSALBOS. Eglise romane avec une tour remarquable ainsi que son portique. Statue romane de N. D. de la Sierra. A 18 Km. de Ségovie.

TUREGANO. Sa fameuse place à portiques est très remarquable, dominée par un magnifique château reconstruit par l'Evêque de Ségovie, D. Juan Arias Dávila au XVe s. Cette forteresse fut la prison du secrétaire de Philippe II, Antonio Pérez.

VILLACASTIN. Magnifique temple de style herrérien, oeuvre de Fray Antonio de Villacastín, contremaître des travaux de l'Escorial. Remarquables retable et peintures de Alonso de Herrera. Auberge Nationale de la Route. A 33 Km. de Ségovie, sur la route générale Madrid-La Coruña.

THE MOST INTERESTING PLACES IN THE PROVINCE

AYLLON. Town whith was once on the estates of Don Alvaro de Luna. Medieval walls. Romanic church, ruined castle; picturesque square.

CARBONERO EL MAYOR. Notable Gothic church, with three naves. lovely altarpiece and magnificent paintings attributed to Rosales, 26 Km. from the capital.

CASTILLO DE CASTILNOVO. Notable medieval castle, undoubtedly the one in the best state of preservation in the province. Privately owned.

COCA. Impressive medieval castle, built by the Fonseca family, in the Mudéjar style. Today Forestry Commissioners' College. Interesting Gothic style church, magnificent tombs of the Fonseca family, carved in alabaster. 48 Km. from the capital.

CUELLAR. Castle-palace built by Don Beltrán de la Cueva in 1464. The town has some interesting Mudéjar churches, remains of the wals, blazoned houses, etc.

EL ESPINAR. Herrerian style church, built by Juan de Minjares; good Plateresque altarpiece; lovely pictures by Sánchez Coello. 35 Km. from the capital.

FUENTIDUEÑA. Picturesque town with the remains of its romanic walls and interesting church in the same style.

LA GRANJA DE SAN ILDEFONSO. Marvellous palace and garden, built by Philip V in 1720, according to plans by Ardemans. The palace houses once of the best tapestry collections in the world.

Palace visiting hours:

From 10 a. m. to 1. p. m. and from 2 p. m. to 6 p. m.

Entrance, fee: Ptas. 20.

Entrance to the garden is fee, except on Thursday, Sundays and holidays from May to October; on these days the prices will be ptas. 15 from 2 p. m.; some of the fountains will be playing. The fountains only play altogether on the following days: 30th May, first Sunday in July and 25th July. Price: 5 ptas. 25th August, festival of San Luis of France, free, 12 Kms. from Segovia on the Madrid road via Navacerrada.

MADERUELO. Town situated in a picturesque spot in the mountains, close to the Linares reservoir and the Riaza river, with abundant fish. Hermitage of Veracruz, which had some magnificent Romanic paintings, and which can be seen today in the Prado Museum in Madrid.

MARTIN MUÑOZ DE LAS POSADAS. Gothic church with an interesting tomb of Cardinal Espinosa and a famous El Greco painting. Remains of the Cardinal's palace.

TERMILLO OBSERVATION POST. Situated 2 Km. from the capital on the Valladolid road. A wonderful view of Segovia.

PEDRAZA. Picturesque walled town with only one gate of access. The Plaza Mayor is one of the most characteristic in Castile. Interesting medieval castle. There is a plan to convert the latter into a National Tourist Parador. 37 Km. from Segovia.

PINAR DE NAVA FRIA. One of the most spectacular pine forests in Spain. 30 Km. from the Capital on the road from the mountains to Riaza.

RIAZA. Summer resort, because of its lovely mountain situation. Typical porticoed square and renaissance parish church. 72 Km. from Segovia.

RIOFRIO. Royal Palace, which Isabel de Farnesio had built when her son Fernando IV succeeded to the throne. The neo-classical style palace has a good collection of paintings including a recently identified Velázquez entitled «The stag's horn» Lovely collection of tapestries. Beautiful park with deer. A cynegetics Museum is to be opened there shortly. 10 Km. from the capital.

SANTA MARIA LA REAL DE NIEVA. Interesting Gothic church, with a transitonal Romanic Gothic cloister. Altarpiece in the style of Berruguete. 30 Km. from Segovia.

SEPULVEDA. Situated in a picturesque spot, surrounded by the Duratón and Castilla rivers. The town itself has a peculiar medieval air, with its blazoned houses, doors in the walls, corners, interesting churches, such as San Justo, San Bartolomé, la Virgen de la Peña and the ruins of the castle. 60 Km. from the capital.

SOTOSALBOS. Romanic church with lovely tower and doorway. Romanic statue of Our Lady of the Mountains. 18 Km. from Segovia.

TUREGANO. It is famous for its porticoed square, with a magnificent castle towering above, rebuilt by the Bishop of Segovia, Don Juan Arias Dávila, in the 15th century. This fortress was used as a prison for Philip II's secretary, Antonio Pérez.

VILLACASTIN. Magnificent Herrerian style church, the work of Friar Antonio de Villacastín, overseer during the built of El Escorial. Interesting altarpiece and paintings by Alonso de Herrera. National Highway Inn. 33 Km. from Segovia on the main Madrid-La Coruña road.

DEPORTES PRINCIPALES

MONTAÑISMO. La proximidad de la Sierra del Guadarrama facilita en buena medida la práctica de los deportes de la nieve y de la montaña. La Sociedad Deportiva Excursionista organiza cada año competiciones de esquí y colabora en las que organizan otras Sociedades madrileñas. Todos los domingos, durante la temporada invernal, hay un servicio de autocar dispuesto por dicha Sociedad a Navacerrada, pudiéndose hacer el viaje también en ferrocarril. En los meses de primavera y verano se realizan excursiones, marchas y competiciones de montaña.

SPORTS PRINCIPAUX

ALPINISME. La proximité de la Sierra de Guadarrama facilite la pratique des sports d'hiver et de l'alpinisme. La Société Sportive Excursionniste organise chaque année des compétitions de ski et collabore à celles qu'organisent les autres sociétés madrilènes. Tous les dimanches, pendant la saison d'hiver, il y a un service d'autocars disposé par cette société vers Navacerrada; le voyage peut également se faire en chemin de fer.

Au printemps et en été on réalise des

excursions, des marches et des compé-
titions d'alpinisme.

MAIN SPORTS

MOUNTAIN SPORTS. Proximity to the Guadarrama Mountain Range makes it easy to
practice winter sports and mountain activities. La Sociedad Deportiva Excursionista
each year organizes ski competitions and
takes part in the sporting activities sponsored
by other Madrid organizations. Every Sunday
in winter, this Society sponsors bus service to Navacerrada. The trip can also be
made by train.
In spring and summer there are tours, hikes
and competitions in the mountains.

COLECCION

«GUÍAS ARTÍSTICO-TURÍSTICAS EVEREST»

GALARDONADA CON EL «TROFEO A LA MEJOR COLECCIÓN TURÍSTICA» EN LA I EXPOSICIÓN BIBLIOGRÁFICA DE SANTANDER

TODAS LAS GUÍAS HAN SIDO DECLARADAS «LIBRO DE INTERÉS TURÍSTICO» POR EL M. DE INFORMACIÓN Y TURISMO

ALAVA
ALBACETE
ALICANTE
ALMERIA
ANDORRA
ASTURIAS
AVILA
BADAJOZ
BARCELONA
BARCELONA, LA PROVINCIA DE
BENIDORM
BURGOS
CACERES
CADIZ
CANTE Y BAILE FLAMENCO
CASTELLON
CASTILLOS DE ESPAÑA
CIUDAD REAL
CORDOBA
COSTA BRAVA
COSTA DEL SOL
CUENCA
DANZAS ESPAÑOLAS
EL CAMINO DE SANTIAGO
EL PARQUE NACIONAL DE ORDESA
EL PIRINEO CATALAN
EL PIRINEO NAVARRO ARAGONES
GERONA
GRAN CANARIA, LANZAROTE, FUERTEVEN-
  TURA
GRANADA
GUADALAJARA
HOSTAL REYES CATOLICOS
HOSTAL DE SAN MARCOS
HUELVA
HUESCA
IBIZA Y FORMENTERA
JAEN
LA CAZA EN ESPAÑA
LA MANCHA TIERRA DE DON QUIJOTE
LA PESCA EN ESPAÑA

LA CORUÑA
LEON
LEON, LA PROVINCIA DE
LERIDA
LISBOA
LOGROÑO
LOS PICOS DE EUROPA
EL MUNDO DE LOS TOROS
LUGO
MADRID
MADRID, LA PROVINCIA DE
MALAGA
MALLORCA
MENORCA
MURCIA
MUSEOS DE MADRID:
  Tomo I: El MUSEO DEL PRADO
  Tomo II: OTROS MUSEOS
NAVARRA
ORENSE
PALENCIA
PARADOR NACIONAL CONDE GONDOMAR
PLASENCIA
PONTEVEDRA: RIAS BAJAS
SALAMANCA
SAN SEBASTIAN Y GUIPUZCOA
SANTANDER
SANTIAGO DE COMPOSTELA
SEGOVIA
SEVILLA
SORIA
TARRAGONA
TENERIFE
TERUEL
TOLEDO
VALENCIA
VALLADOLID
VIGO Y SU RIA
VIZCAYA
ZAMORA
ZARAGOZA

EDICIONES en Español - Francés - Inglés - Alemán - Sueco - Italiano y Portugués.

(Para una mayor información consulte nuestro Catálogo general)